Preparation for
Marriage

William & Stephanie Brock

CONTENTS

PREPARATION FOR MARRIAGE

SECTIONS

STARTING A FIRM FOUNDATION IN MARRIAGE - SECTION 1

1. The Culture of America
2. We Have to Be Taught
3. Roles are Defined
4. Right Perspectives
5. Scripture for God's Plan For Marriage
6. Points from The Song of Solomon
7. Types of Love
8. The Difference Between Men and Women
9. Preparation for Marriage
10. Prayer
11. Love and Respect
12. Women! Respect Your Husband
13. Men! Love Your Wife
14. Watch What You Wear or Don't Wear
15. For Better or Worse
16. No Time for Wars
17. Intimacy and Bonding
18. Leaving and Cleaving
19. Don't Be Unequally Yoked
20. Be an Encourager, Not a Discourager
21. Dump the Baggage Into the Dumpster
22. Problems with Releasing
23. The Covering
24. Practicality and Organization
25. Priorities Must Be Defined
26. Avoid Negative Character Traits
27. What Type of Effort are You Going to Put Forth

THE CULTURE OF AMERICA

The group of people who are in control of this country have purposely divided people up and put them in certain social grouping. People have been brainwashed because of where they live, because of their race, or because of their economic status. Most poor people don't think like the rich people and many underprivileged people don't like influential people. Why? Simply because the influential want to keep the underprivileged dumb by keeping them away from information that would be very valuable to help them. Distractions are set up to keep them from investing in themselves, such as pornography, violent TV shows, sports, gambling, lotteries or long working hours. The wrong messages are being sent by the very same elected officials we have placed in leadership, which are guiding our children to seeing the wrong type of role models. When you isolate a society into certain ungodly thought patterns, it certainly creates problems that are brought about like time bombs toward society's destructions.

Sex is and has always been a very big deal in society when it's about to fall. There are more open perversions that are accepted today. Homosexuality, is not an alternative lifestyle, it is an abomination before God and should not be accepted and looked upon as a good thing as Christians. We are to love the sinner, but hate the sin. Adultery is not playing around, it is a sin against God which brings His chastisement upon the persons involved. It is time for us to start calling everything just as it is, sin is sin. Immorality is running rampant, and every indecent thing that can be thought of, it looks like it is happening today.

The real scary thing is that sins are being accepted by a lot of Christians. Where is the outrage for half of the marriages within the church ending in divorce, or the millions of abortions that are performed in America every year, and the many church leaders who are caught in adulterous affairs? The world has come into the church and no one is telling the people "we can't go along with what is popular in the world", "we have to go by the word of God as it is written", "and we can't tolerate sin under the disguise of grace and expect God to go along with it".

WE HAVE TO BE TAUGHT

The right things must be taught by the right people or the family is headed for destruction. Christians must be Christ controlled, and not flesh controlled. Safe sex is husband and wife period. We have to start taking our covenant with God and each other seriously.

A gentle touch and a soft response wins respect. Learn to enjoy each other and have discretion. Your mate doesn't want you going around showing your body to everyone or telling about your intimate experiences with anyone.

There was once a time when a woman was called a floozy, Jezebel, or worse, if they went out of their home with their skirts up to their behind, or if they walked outside with see through clothing, or if their clothing was so tight that it looked as if it was painted on, or you can see every bulge, and contour of their body.

Men are wearing earrings in both ears, makeup and cross dressing, going to the beauty salon to get hair weaves, and have manicures and pedicures. They are out there in the world having sex with any and everyone who is willing. Some of these men are leaders in our churches and our country. Color does not have a determining factor on these statements. These men have no morals, sense of right or wrong, dignity, shame or discretion.

Women, you are the major key in your husband's life. His affirmation as a man will come from his wife, the major influence in his life other than Christ. Why is it that we never hear anything about sensual attraction within a marriage of a man and woman? Attention is always focused on affairs, same sex marriages and partnerships, and not on the traditional marriage. If women would prepare a few enticements for their husbands, he will take the initiative and respond. But spouses need to have some spice (excitement) in their sex life. But if the man is hard working and drained by the end of the day, you had better believe he will need some help to feel good about himself. Wives, you are the helper. Wives you should know what your husband desires and help him to achieve those desires, as you are helping him, he should be pleasuring you also.

ROLES ARE DEFINED

In the Bible, the roles of men and women, husbands and wives, are clearly defined. The man is supposed to go out and work hard, and the woman is to take care of the home front. Marriage is one man and one woman, coordinating the family activities together. The world today is sending messages that men are bumbling idiots, and the women need to take over to keep the family going. Just like in the Garden of Eden. Where did that take us?

The man is supposed to be the head of his household, leading the family in God's direction. Women are supposed to let the man lead by being submissive. Becoming one flesh, usually, is not a natural thing that just comes about. It has to be molded, and shaped, and worked at. And remember, men think more differently than women do. So you have to know for a fact, what your role is. The movements which are trying to redefine the functions of males and females, sexually and psychologically, are truly wrong, and have been cleverly conceived. Men have not been given the ok to have sexual encounters with men, and neither have women with women, by God's authority.

Ladies, if you can't follow the leadership of a husband, don't get married. The man is the heard of the family because God said so. Either you honor that, or you get into the sin of disobedience. Men, you are to love you wife unconditionally, to protect her at all times as she is the weaker vessel. Ladies, seek a meek and humble spirit, to promote peace in your household.

Scripture References:

Genesis 3:15-16, 23
1 Peter 3:1-10

RIGHT PERSPECTIVES

If your spouse doesn't have the second place in your life after Christ, you're heading down the wrong path. There should always be an order of respect and responsibility in a home. In this day and time, it's difficult to establish the proper husband and wife bond because of the improper programing of the way people tend to think, which carries over to their priorities in life. There has to be a commitment to God first, your spouse second, your children and family third, then your job and other activities, in that order. Marriage is a commitment, for better or worse, until death do you part. Not just when you feel like putting forth an effort toward a commitment.

Today, some people take their marriage vows just as words. The vows should be taken serious, just not when it's convenient. It is not the way God sees it, to Him it is a lifelong vow, not only to your marriage partner, but to Him also, and that should never be broken.

Don't assume that your spouse automatically knows what you want or like, or knows what happened to you in your past, or even knows what you want for your future. Sharing yourself is critical in a marriage that works, we have to learn how. Many times, some of the problems you will have in your marriage, are some of the same sort of unresolved problems you have with God. If we get right with God our other problems will fall in line, when we learn how to trust God, we will learn how to trust our marriage partner. There is a little game that some spouse's play with their partner, that we will call "accommodation by separation". This is when one partner thinks they are doing their partner a favor, by purposely keeping themselves separated from the other, because that one thinks they are too fat, not pretty enough, too stupid, or any other excuse.

This is a strange way of thinking and it just doesn't quite cut it in God's program. Marriage is for better or worse, regardless of what anyone says, and you can't cleave if you are separated.

There is definitely a difference between the charms of a worldly man or woman, and the charms of a Godly wife or husband. The charms of the world, as the lust of the flesh, the lust of the eyes, and the pride of life, which allure men and women in the wrong direction, away from lasting relationships with each other. The charms of a Godly wife toward her husband, attracts and can never be overlooked by him. These are the things that are not being taught to the younger women by the older women today, (Titus 2:3-5) and the families are paying for it.

How can we become overcomers, feel good about ourselves, or have a growing relationship with our mates, if we can't get over our past? We have to remember who we are in Christ. Feelings of inadequacy or shame, have to be nailed to the cross of Jesus Christ. Jesus did not die for us to feel inferior, but to lift Him up in all things.

Scripture References:

Matthew 5:31-33, 9:4-9

Hebrews 13:4

1 Corinthians 7:2-16, 13:4-7

Ephesians 5:21-33

Mark 10:6-12

SCRIPTURES FOR GOD'S PLAN
FOR MARRIAGE

Old Testament

Genesis 2:23-25, 3:16-23
Proverbs 5:18-19

New Testament

Matthew 19:3-9
Romans 1:26-27
1 Corinthians 7:1-16, 27-34, 11:3, 8-15
2 Corinthians 6:14
Galatians 5:19-26
Ephesians 5:21-33
Colossians 2:2, 3:12-14, 18-19
1 Thessalonians 4:11, 5:22,
1 Timothy 2:9-15, 5:8, 13-15
2 Timothy 3:1-7
Titus 2:2-8
Hebrews 13:4, 17
James 1:26, 3:14-16
1 Peter 3:1-12

Love

1 Corinthians 13
1 John 2:9-11, 3:10-11, 14-18, 23, 4:7-13, 18, 20-21, 5:2-3

POINTS FROM THE BOOK
SONG OF SOLOMON

Chapter 1:7

Make your wife feel secure with your presence.

A. Commitment is the basis of true love

B. Genuine live eliminates fear of deceit, manipulation, or exploitation.

Chapter 2:1

Encouragement and appreciation is vital to the person you love. Tell your spouse, "I Love You" every day and show that you love them by your actions.

Chapter 2:7

Feelings of love can create intimacy that overpowers reason. Patiently wait for feelings of love and commitment to development together.

Chapter 2:16

Belonging to your spouse is not the same as possessing each other, allow your mate some room.

Chapter 3:1-4

When you love someone, you will do all you can to ensure the safety of that other person and care for his or her needs, even at the cost of your own personal comfort. This shows up most often in small action sacrificing your own personal comfort to tend to the needs of the ones you love.

Chapter 4:1-7

Communicating love and expressing admiration in both words and actions can enhance every marriage.

Chapter 4:15

Do you refresh your spouse, or are you a burden of complaints, sorrows and problems? Partners in marriage should continually work at refreshing each other by an encouraging word, an unexpected gift, a change of pace, a surprise call or note, or even a withholding of a discussion of a problem until the proper time.

Chapter 5:2

Couple's marriages should grow and mature in spite of problems. Self-centeredness and impatience can cause problems. Quickly move to correct problems.

Chapter 5:2-7

Take the time to remember the first thrills, the excitement of sex, your spouse's strengths, and the commitment you made to one another. When you focus on the positives, reconciliation and renewal can result.

Chapter 5:16

A deep friendship takes time, and includes listening, sharing, and showing understand for the other person's likes and dislikes. It makes a love relationship much deeper and far more satisfying.

Chapter 6:3

Married people belong to each other, and must give themselves to each other unreservedly. In marriage they should complete union of mind, heart, and body.

Chapter 7:10-13

As a marriage matures, there should be more love and freedom between partners. Here, the woman takes initiative in lovemaking. Many cultures have stereotypes of the roles that men and women play in lovemaking, but the security of true love gives both marriage partners equality and the freedom to initiate acts of love and express their true feelings.

Chapter 8:6-7

Love is as strong as death, it cannot be contained and it cannot be bought for any price, because it is given freely. Love is priceless, and even the richest king cannot buy it.

Chapter 8:11-12

In marriage there is no private property, because everything is shared between partners.

Chapter 8:14

Love should not diminish in intensity after the wedding night. Lovers should rely on each other and keep no secrets from each other. Devotion and commitment are keys to the relationship. The faithfulness of our marital love should reflect God's perfect faithfulness to us.

TYPES OF LOVE

1. Eros
2. Storge
3. Philia
4. Agape
5. Ludus
6. Pragma
7. Philautia
8. Mania

Eros love is sexual or passionate love, and is the type most akin to our modern construct of romantic love

Storge love is a slow developing, friendship-based love

Philia love is close friendship or brotherly love

Agape love is unconditional. No matters what happen, this type of love never stops. We must have faith in God to be able to release Agape love.

Agape love in the marriage and family is what holds it all together through all kinds of seasons. It's the selfless, unconditional type of love that helps people to forgive one another, to respect one another, and to serve one another, day in and day out.

Ludus love is playful love. Having many conquests but remaining uncommitted.

Pragma love is a pragmatic, practical, mutually beneficial relationship.

Philautia love is self-love; self-conceit; undue regard for oneself or one's own interests.

Mania love is an obsessive or possessive love, jealous and extreme.

THE DIFFERENCE BETWEEN
MEN AND WOMEN

MEN

The top five emotional needs of men are:

1. Sexual fulfillment
2. Recreational companionship
3. Physical attractiveness of their mate
4. Domestic support
5. Admiration for their mate

Characteristics of Men

1. Men use the left side of the brain which mean they think from logic.

2. Men remover very little from day to day unless they keep records

3. Men get turned on by their wives by what he see, smells and hears. In other words if your wife has a problem with showing her body to her husband, there may develop a problem in the marriage.

4. Men limit their conversations to very current events.

5. Many men think they can use their money, prestige, or power to get a woman.

6. Men are drawn by rough and rugged activities (sports, (playing or watching), camping, fishing, etc.

7. Most men don't really see reason for romancing, so they would rather just jump into bed.

8. A makes role is to seek out the female. Men today in America (in many cases) are wimps. No one expects them to be perfect, but they have had a steady downhill slide since Adam

allowed Eve to take control of the Garden.

9. Men have got to learn how to strengthen their wife's character by being a positive influence. Men have to be a steward over your wife for God and learn to be an inspirational leader. Acknowledge your wife's sensitivities, as being the weaker vessel (physically, emotionally, etc.) be the backbone.

10. The man is the priest of his home. Setting the morals of his home through scripture.

WOMEN

The top five emotional needs of women are:

1. Affection
2. Conversation
3. Honesty and openness
4. Financial support
5. Family commitment

Characteristics of Women

1. Women use the right side of their head which means they think from emotion

2. Women remember details from years back

3. Women get turned on by touch and what effects them emotionally. Husbands, learn to romantic quickly.

4. Women love to talk about anything and everything.

5. Many women think they can use their beauty (bodies) to get a man.

6. Women are drawn to activities that revolve around the home.

7. Most women want to be romanced instead of just jumping into bed.

8. A woman's role is to attract and respond. Many modern day

American women have not learned how to be virtuous, exalted, faithful, tender, loyal devoted, compassionate, toward their own husbands, such as many women in other cultures. But these are character traits that have got to be taught from examples. This is another reason for dissension within the family. Many mothers are not teaching their daughters how to be wives, they are teaching them how to be rebels. Wives are honoring everyone but their husbands. It is truly a blessing to have a wife that is feminine, and has a meek and humble spirit.

9. Wives need to give their husbands an affirming lift to his manhood, and learn how to do this. Wives, your relationship with your husband is going to show through him wherever he goes. If you don't build him up, he will probably be a very downtrodden person.

10. The woman is her man's cheerleader to push him on.

PREPARATION FOR MARRIAGE

Agape Love 1 Corinthians 13

This chapter is declaring love to be the greatest attribute that a man can display. It give the character of true love in action. If a person can achieve a heart filled with love, they would truly be in touch with God's Spirit. There are several character traits that are in opposition to love.

Jealousy, boastfulness, pride, rudeness, people demanding to have their own way, being irritable, keeping record of being wronged, rejoicing about injustice, giving up and losing faith.

Strife-conflicts between people, envy-resentment against another person's success, dissension-quarreling, self-conceit-an exaggerated opinion of yourself, provoking one another-to anger or irritate, rudeness-discourteous, impolite, ill-mannered. We must decrease in self, and increase in show the Love of God.

But it says that love is patient and kind, it rejoices whenever the truth wins out, and it is hopeful and endures through every circumstance. It last forever and is the greatest of all attributes for men to possess. It is sacrificial love.

PRAYER

We have to be in constant prayer for our spouses. If there is something in them we don't like, we must pray to God to look at ourselves as we may be the one at fault. If God shows us that we are not in fault, then ask God to show you what is needed to change to make your marriage to be a good one. Marriages are always under consistent attacks from every side possible. But you must take the time to thank God for whom He has blessed you with. Pray and ask that the Lord will bless your spouse throughout the day when you are going your separate ways to work, shop, or whatever the case may be. Ask God to keep them protected and to also give them special favor with their boss, co-workers, associates, and clients. Also ask that will be used mightily by God for His purpose. God should be asked to bless our goings out, and the coming in. Interceding for our spouses is a tremendous blessing for the whole family.

Scripture References:

Luke 18:1
James 5:6
1 Peter 3:7

LOVE AND RESPECT

God has commanded men to love their wives, and command women to respect their husbands. What does this mean?

Men you are the leader, it's up to you to make the ultimate sacrifice of agape love for your wife. Agape love is unconditional, never ending, life surrendering love that has no strings attached. It just goes on and on and on, like the ever ready bunny. No matter what happens, it just keeps going. Like Christ love the Church enough to make the ultimate sacrifice of His life. Men are to love their wives that much. Even when your wife is unlovable, you are to love them anyway. Men are to treat their wives, like their favorite hobby or their cars, their guns, their collectables, or any other things they cherish so dearly with tender loving care.

No matter what the feminist may say, the wife is the weaker vessel, and the husband has to be her strength. The only person to lift her up and to make her feel like the queen of his life. Not a dumpster for cursing at or to put down, not a punching bag to make you feel better about your inadequacy of your manhood. It doesn't take a real man to slap a woman around. But it does take a real man to lead and guide her, to make her feel like a special lady.

Elder men of the church, should teach the younger men how to love their wives. How to be a living sacrifice for God's Glory, in their marriage. Chivalry is not dead, and we must teach our young men how to be a gentleman. Very Quickly!!!!!

Women, you are to be the helper, just as God created you to be. You are commanded to honor and respect your husband. Sarah honored Abraham by calling him lord. Remember that your husband is your head, and your protector. He is the bread winner of the household. In most cases, he fixes what must be fixed. If you have a husband like this, don't you think he deserves your uttermost respect? He may not do the things the way you want them done, or when you want them done, or even when you want it done, but he does get things done. Sometimes there are more important things that must take place before he can do what you want done.

The number one way a woman can dishonor her husband is with her mouth. You can kill a man's self-worth, with nagging, putdowns, cursing at him, bringing up his past faults. There are many cases when a woman wants to get back at her husband by withholding sex, not cooking, sleeping in a separate room, not talking, avoiding eye contact, even avoid being in the same room. When a woman feels like she has been hurt, it usually goes deeply into her heart. She may forget that getting back at her husband will curse the marriage and their family. If she is out of fellowship with God, then she will not pray, and that will open doors for evil to come into the home. This is how divorces come about, when the thinking process has been distorted. Remember men and women don't think alike most of the time.

Many Christian people tend to forget Christians don't return evil for evil, or this is our lifelong marriage partner, for better or for worse. We forget we are supposed to be one flesh, and what effects one, will affect the whole family. Breaking the marriage vows is definitely a sin.

People of God have to grow up spiritually and put your feelings aside to look toward Jesus. It hurt Jesus, when every one of His disciples turned away from Him when He was put on trial for His life, but Jesus knew who He was and what He had to do.

Women have to learn how to appease a man's ego, in order to accomplish God's best for the family. This is why the bible says the older women should teach the younger women, for them to know how to create an atmosphere of respect for their husbands, and to draw him by her quiet, meek and humble spirit. This will work the majority of the time, whether the man is saved or not.

Wives, give your husband's something to pursue. If they don't see you exciting, they probably won't chase after you. If you don't give your husband something to visualize of how fantastic you are, they will forget. A man usually gets turned off, if you deny him of your body, visually and physically. This is what most men thrive off of and look forward to from their wives. Wives, you should be the main attraction to draw your husband home every day. Many men will tell their friends, coworkers, etc., "no way will I hang out, I have someone at home waiting for me". Wives, make home worth coming home to. Have the house clean, dinner cooking, clothes cleaned, be dressed and looking nice, if you don't work, but if you do, there should be an even medium for you. You come home from work, and cook dinner, and make your husband feel good to be home. If you want your husband to focus on you, then you must give him something to see and remember. There is something left to his imagination, and his imagination should be set on you, his wife.

There are quite a few things young women who are married are missing out on, and they should be able to go to the older women of the church, the church mothers to learn from. Young married women who want to stay married, should not be ashamed to go to them for counsel, this is needed if you want your marriage to be strong and to last.

Scripture References:

Titus 2:2-8
1 Peter 3:1-12, 5:5
Ephesians 5:21-33
Proverbs 12:4

WOMEN RESPECT YOUR HUSBANDS

Many women in this day and time, have a very disrespectful manner of speaking to their husbands, and they think its ok. But it's definitely not. When you and your husband are out in the public and speaking to him like he's a dog, this is just utterly disrespectful, to him, to the people around him, and to you. A man does not need his wife to make him look like a fool. But if she does, if reflects directly back on her, and the people around are asking the questions of, "why is she even with this man, or why is he still with her?" If you make him look bad, you will definitely look bad yourself.

If you don't know how to encourage your husband, seek some Godly counsel. Don't take your husband for granted. You may turn away, while someone else is watching, wanting and waiting.

Women, if you want to be sexy, be sexy at home for your husband and not out in the streets. If you want to dress provocatively, do it at home, because you will only make yourself look like a street walker, and that is definitely disrespecting your husband. If you are not sure how to dress, or what you will look nice in, ask your husband, because it is him who you want to please. If your husband is not saved, then of course, you will not want to ask him, because he may like for you to look like a street walker. A saved husband, and you as a saved woman, will dressed godly, and will also, have your pants loose, dress or skirt over your knees, your bosom covered. Everything on your body is not for the world to see, but only for your husband. This is another reason why godly church mothers need to be sought for guidance.

Disrespect brings forth animosity, separation, and unrest. Resentment for your husband will linger if not taken care of. Because the relationship has been severed. Christians are not in the business of tearing people down, but lifting them up. If you cannot do that for your husband, then you should not get married. Marriage is more than a relationship, it's a bond between two people, to be happy. Yes you will have some down time, but it's up to you if you started it, to end it, and to make up. This is the same for the husband. Always be willing to go a little extra to make your husband happy, because it will also make you happy.

Remember ladies, a man is not going to stay with a woman who continually disrespects him, and constantly dogs him out. He has enough problems in the world without coming home to unnecessary arguments, and problems.

Wives remember, building up your husband is building you up also.

Scripture References:

1 Peter 3:1-6
Titus 2:4
Proverbs 12:4
Ephesians 5:22-24
1 Timothy 2:9-15
1 Corinthians 3:1-6

MEN LOVE YOUR WIFE

What is unconditional love (agape love) for your wife?

It means sacrificial love, going through any condition which might come about. The world's love never last. It says if you don't measure up, you are out. But God's love never quits and never ends. This is the type of love God wants a husband to have for his wife. If a man loves his wife, he will love himself.

Men be willing to help your wife. If she calls on you to help her, don't do it begrudgingly because that will set off problems that could have been avoided. If she asks you to do something at a certain time, and you cannot do it at that time, be willing to communicate those facts to her. Open communication extracts greater love and respect for each other.

Compliment her on things that she has worked hard to please you with. It will make her want to do more. Let her know she is appreciated and that you love her. If she is not a great cook but tries anyway. Again, open communication is the key to making her feel good about at least trying. Women hurt easily and it's up to you men, to keep from hurting her, but to show love and keep it real. Make her always feel she is the only woman for you.

Scripture References:

1 Peter 4:7
Ephesians 5:25-29, 31-33
Colossians3:19
1 John 4:7-12
1 Corinthians 7:4-5

WATCH WHAT YOU WEAR, OR DON'T WEAR

Women, just knowing the difference between men and women, you are going to have more of a problem with this than the men. Men scope in on women, it's in their nature. So women, if you have on a tight mini skirt or a dress with a split way up too far, or a blouse that is opened too far down, tight and showing cleavage, you are definitely drawing trouble to yourself. Why do you think they show lingerie commercials on TV? Why do you think they show women in bikinis or in skimpy clothing? Why do they show men in speedo's and skimpy clothes or even bare

chested? They are purposely trying to draw men and women from their spouses for the bucks.

If you want to wear sexy clothing or sexy underwear, do it at home to arouse your spouse. You can entice your mate at the right time and right place. You need to always wear appropriate clothing when you are out in public. Do not bring disrespect to yourself by the way you dress. If the people see you dressing provocatively, they will lose respect for you, because you are not respecting yourself.

Scripture References:

1 Peter 3:3
1 Timothy 2:9-10

FOR BETTER OR WORSE,
RICHER OR POORER

Don't do what you already know is against God's Word. You know that you are supposed to be exclusive with your mate, for life. Don't let situations or people turn you against the vows that you have made to your mate and before God. No one is going to make it easy to keep your wedding vows. Find out who the person is before making the commitment, it will save you and your spouse a lot of heartache and pain. But once you have made the commitment and said "I Do", it is a commitment for the rest of your life. But a true fact of today is that there are a lot of con-artists out there, preying on innocent folks, and taking advantage of whomever they think they can get over on. They will talk the talk, but will not walk the walk. So don't be fooled by what it looks like on the outside. Ask God to help you see the person for who they really are, and then you will be able to make the decision. If God shows you that person is not right, and you go on with your plans anyway, you are setting yourself up for problems. But if you leave that person and wait for God to send you another, you will have to wait, but you will be well pleased.

You have to show your spouse that you love them, during good times and bad. Don't show love only when it benefits you and lines up with your standards, or when you think your spouse is deserving. That is not love at all. Remember, God can and will make changes in you and your spouse when you turn to Him. You must always have your spouse's back at all times.

NO TIME FOR WARS

There are enough conflicts in the world, without creating new ones at home. Your spouse will not want to come home if the home is not worth coming home to. There should be peace in the home, not a chaotic atmosphere. Arguing, snapping, cussing, and just being judgmental is not what your spouse wants to come home to, especially if they have a stressful job, or workplace. When a spouse feels their home is going to be filled with chaos, they will chose to hang out after work with some of their friends or colleagues, which only causes more chaos when they do get home. So it's a no win situation. Men want to protect their home, but really can't when their spouse is abusive and argumentive.

Never threaten your spouse because the outcome is never any good. Negotiations are always better than retaliation. You get a lot better reaction with a soft and controlled tone of speech. Building up strife and contention will just not go away. Don't close yourself off to a new way of thinking, be open. The Bible says to be angry, but to sin not. So what does that mean? Ephesians 4:26, says, that you are in order, in control, hearing what is being said, and seeing what is being done. So the question is, do you attack and retaliate, or do you humble yourself and let God hand the situation?

Scripture References:

Proverbs 15:1
James 1:19-21
1 Peter 2:33
Galatians 6:1

INTIMACY AND BONDING

Without a doubt, one of the hardest things to do in today's fast pace, computer tech, society, is to draw closer to one another. How can there be intimacy with so many sidetracks, hang-ups and so many different sources of influence to impact your mind?

First, you have to know what the Word of God is saying and have a handle on the meaning of the passages of scripture you have read. If you learn to draw closer to God He will draw closer to you. After that husbands and wives can draw closer to together.

God has directed us toward sacrifice, submission, servanthood, and humility. These things are contradictory to what the world is promoting today. The Spirit of rebellion is strong upon families today, because we are taking on the values of the world instead of the values of God.

Spouses must not compare their marriage partner with was is seen in a magazine, on the TV, or what you may have imagined or fantasized in your mind, to be a perfect person. Those images are not real. There are no perfect people in this world, but there are no other people in this world like your mate. Accept your mate as they are.

If you have been programmed unbiblically in your thinking, it will affect the way you relate to your spouse and everyone else. It is up to each one as individuals, to learn the biblical way of thinking about yourself, other people, and everyday situations. How can we have a healthy intimate, relationship with our spouse, if we are always suspicious of every action or motive behind the action? Know that you and your spouse are on the same team, and you are drawing closer together for the same cause and that is for Jesus Christ.

LEAVE AND CLEAVE

When two people get married, they have to come to grips that they will have to leave things behind, so they can cleave to each other. But often times, people have problems cutting off ties from mother, father, sister, brother, other relatives and even friends they had before their marriage. Cleaving means to cling to, be glued together, bounded and cannot be separated. But in today's society, many people don't want to give up anything, they want it all as if they were still single. The world is saying it's ok, you can do what you want, just because you got married doesn't mean you should stop living the life you were accustomed to before you got married.

The church is to a large degree accepting much of the world's ways and points of view and marriage is no exception. Just look at the rate of divorce, adultery, homosexuality, abortions, same sex marriage that are being accepted as a lifestyle option within many churches.

You can't cleave to your old fleshly ways of thinking, and at the same time start a new Godly life with your spouse. The world has mixed up many people's priorities, so that many people think that putting kids, mothers, pastors, friends, or relative's first is alright. Well, it's not alright. Your spouse must have priority over everyone except for God. God must be first in your and your spouse's life. You should sever any and every tie that may hinder your loyalty from your spouse. Separate yourself from every obstacle that will lead you away from a bonding relationship with your spouse. It takes time to build a strong inseparable relationship and a very small amount of time to tear it apart.

Are you setting up any type of barriers between you and your spouse? It's terrible when everyone that you want to cling to will try to tear up your marriage including the devil himself. But understand, a husband and wife can destroy their own relationship without the help from anyone or anything outside the marriage.

The Bible says that husbands and wives shall become one flesh, and whomsoever shall try to separate them will be cursed.

Scripture References:

Genesis 2:24, 3:16
Mark 10:7
Ephesians 5:31

DON'T BE UNEQUALLY YOKED

We all have to face the facts that all people are not who they seem to be. This is a day of great deception. So how can we tell if a person is really who they are portraying themselves to be? We have to watch, pray, and listen to the Holy Spirit as he reveals the truth. This is not a day of compassion as it may have been in the past, but a day of getting over on someone to get what they want, and doing whatever it takes to get it. There are bad people out everywhere, trying to trap you, and rip you off of everything you have. They may look good, they may smell good, they may say the right things, and they may even look successful in life. But they may be wolves in sheep clothing. God will allow you to know the true facts, not wishful thinking. I am not saying everyone is perfect, but deception has a pattern and if you close your eyes to that pattern, you will become the sucker.

Christian character is clear in the bible. People straying away from that character has an ongoing habit, and is a sure sign. I am not talking about something such as this person does not cook 7 days a week, or this person watches football every Sunday. I am talking about signs of drug use, excessive drinking, gambling, and disappearing for days and nights at a time without a believable explanation. Just maybe a person has a job, or says they have a job, but never have any money. These are typical signs of ungodly character. Hanging around with the wrong people, keeping secrets and not being honest are bad signs. If there is no consistent growth of any type of Godly character, leave them alone.

Scripture References:

Hebrews 4:12, 5:14   2 Corinthians 6:14

Malachi 3:18   1 Thessalonians 5:6

Matthew 10:16-24   Acts 20:29-31

1 Peter 4:7

1 Corinthians 2:14

BE AN ENCOURAGER - NOT A DISCOURAGER

Don't let a cloud of discouragement fall on your marriage. Learn how to receive a compliment as well as how to give a compliment. Show appreciation for positive comments or renderings of compassion. Don't let your spouse think that their encouragement has fallen on deaf ears. It is considerate to give positive affirmation and responses for what your spouse does for you. Take the time to say, "thank you for making me feel special". Your mate is looking at from an opposite sex perspective, that you may not be able to see in yourself. Let them esteem your personal attributes, without blowing up your head. You say something along the lines of "praise God" or a "thank you", or maybe more like, "you really thinks so", when your spouse compliments you. The Bible says to be kindly affectionate one toward another.

Wrong attitudes are some of the major discouragers in a marriage. Just imagine if a husband brought a dozen roses to his wife, and when he gives them to her, she would in a negative way say, "I don't feel like roses today, just throw them in the trash." Another scenario, a wife goes out and gets herself all fancied up with a sheer, sexy nightgown, and she comes to her husband looking like a million dollars, and she asks him to go to bed early all he can say to her, "I have a lot of work to finish up before the night, so I may just sleep on the couch". How does that make each other feel? Harshness in actions or words hurt who they are directed to. Jesus showed compassion to the people that were around Him, even to the people He didn't know. We all need learn how to release a caring, sensitive, heart for our spouse and for others.

Comparing your spouse to someone else, to let them know that they just don't quite measure up, is a blatant act of a lack of compassion or love. Nagging, complaining, cursing, gossiping about how bad your spouse is, brings about animosity between the two of you. You just don't say some things to or about your marriage partner, because when you do, you are also saying something very negative about yourself.

Many people today are still trying to explain why they don't have intimacy within their marriage. Couples who have been married for twenty or more years are just living together and not loving as they did before, because no one want to admit that there is a problem. Many of them are deeply discouraged because of secrets that have been withheld from earlier years, or a rape, abuse of any or all types, which bring problems into the marriage. It is not wise to continue to hold on to these types of problems without trying to get some help from a Christian counselor. If counseling is not sought, it will only hurt the marriage.

Women, if you have a problem with your husband viewing or massaging your body, you may run into a problem with your marriage. Men are made by God to admire the attractiveness of his mate, with his eyes, touch and smell. A man is going to feel rejected if he is not given this trust by his wife.

Women thrive on communication, those romantic, sensitive, moments that touch their hearts (emotions). If your wife does not feel like you care what is going on in her life, then husbands you are going to have problems. This is why sometimes women are drawn to other men, because someone else will listen, care and show affection when you have stopped. Husbands you need to pay attention to the needs of your wives, to make her feel like she is a part of your life.

Men, if you have a problem with your wife, if she doesn't touch you the right way or arouse you, you may need to talk to her or to teach her. Many women have a hard time with touching their men because of past experiences. But if your wife is a virgin, then you will have to teach her because she will have no knowledge of how to please her man by not having a previous relationship before you.

Misunderstandings start with ignorance of facts. The magnetism between a husband and his wife is definitely given by God, but sometimes it must be energized through understanding.

The ministry of marriage is truly a mystery in today's world, because people are unwilling or unable to give a total sacrifice of themselves to their marriage partner. In either case, spouses need to turn lives over to God, to learn the truth to set them free. There are too many case within a marriage where the main problem is too much of me, myself, and I and not enough of we, ourselves and us. There is also not enough compromising, only the "I'll do this for you if you do this for me." It should be whenever one asks other to do something that is should be done with a joyful heart and only too happy to do it.

Children growing up under the conditions of discouraging parents have also been affected by uncaring peers, relatives, teachers and adults. But these children have to know what the attacks from uncaring people of the past only built miser in their own adult lives. When problems arose from the parents, the children were the first to get the rough end of it all, so this is considered as a generational curse that misery and mistreatment is carried on from generation to generation. In order for this curse to be broken you must become the son or daughter of God that He created you to be, that may be able to be an encourager of others and it starts with your family.

DUMP THE BAGGAGE IN THE DUMPSTER

There are plenty of heavy baggage situations (burdens), that people bring into their marriages today. It truly complicates a relationship. There are broken families, violence, psychological problems, sociological problems, etc. You are going to have to be able to release yourself first to God, then to your spouse. Holding onto the past will be over when you get married. That is, if you want to stay married. Any past injustices should be handed over to Jesus Christ to be nailed to the cross. I know that some situations have been very difficult, but I know someone who can solve any problem you may have, and He is Jesus Christ. Remember, we are all dysfunctional in one way or another, because of the sin in this world. But Jesus overcame all things, even death.

Scripture References:

Hebrews 12:1
James 1:21

PROBLEMS WITH RELEASING

Some people are unable to release their own bodies, over to their mates, because of past issues of trust that have gone unresolved. Solve that problem or you will never be close to your mate. No confidence in yourself, will also cause you to have no confidence in anyone else. What excuse are you using to deprieve your marriage partner of due benevolence in your relationship? You can't continue to be disobedient in your marriage, and expect God to put is blessing on it.

THE COVERING

The way we define a covering is when a spouse (or a brother or sister of the same sex), wraps their protection around the other spouse (or person) by their presence. Kind of like what the womb is to a baby. This is what the man is supposed to be for the woman at all times. Men, your wife should fill secure in your hands.

Women, your husband wants you to intervene if a woman approaches him for counciling or anything else, that's if he is a man of God. He shouldn't have to holler across a room, if some woman goes up to him to start a conversation with him, ladies, you should be over there faster than wonder woman. We can never linger with anyone of the opposite sex without a covering. Spouses, don't let your husband or wife have to ask you five or six times, to come into counciling sessions with someone of the opposite sex. We have to create an atmosphere of integrity for another.

Scripture References:

Galatians 6:1-2
Romans 15:1

PRACTICALITY AND ORGANIZATION

Whenever you are in a relationship with someone, you have to ask yourself, "is this idea that the other person has, a practical solution for this situation?" We also have to realize that we are in a relationship, which means an US solution, and not a ME solution. We have to recognize that we are doing things for the best interest of the family, which may mean sacrificing what you may want, for a better solution you may never have thought about. We are to become one flesh when you get married, and that may mean yielding to, and giving credit to your spouse. Two different points of view does not have to be detrimental, because planning goals together is part of management in marriage. Yes, that's right, it is a part of becoming one flesh. There is no more "my bank account, and your bank account," no more "mine and yours ", it's ours from now on.

Don't take things so seriously, lay back and work out practical solutions together. Laugh and enjoy each other's input. We are helpers of one another, and we need to demonstrate more of this inside of our homes, before we can demonstrate compassion outside of our homes. Humility is shown through addressing the needs, and showing gratitude for other people. We must create an open atmosphere of consideration of ideas, and support decisions of practicality, for the bonding of your family.

Scripture References:

Romans 12:16
1 Corinthians 1:10, 12:25
Amos 3:3
Philippians 2:2

PRIORITES MUST BE DEFINED

In marriage, certain priorities have to take precedence over other. The wife or the husband comes first, before you go outside the home to take of business. Then the children, then other family members or acquaintances. Not your buddies or your mama first.

Now on the financial front, we really have to keep focused. You cannot buy a $75,000.00 dollar car, and have $200,000.00 dollar house, when your income is $65,000.00 dollars a year. You cannot smoke packs of cigarettes a day, and drink two six packs of beer, and you don't have any money for gas for your car. You can't go to the casino, or worlds of fun, and you don't have food in your refrigerator. You can't be going to a football game and your wife and kids don't have clothes or shoes to wear.

The bottom line is to take care of home first. You should not be going to clean someone else's house when your house is filthy. You should not go out of your home to take care of someone else when you are not taking care of the people at your own house.

You can't bow down to the pastor's feet when you don't respect your own spouse. You can't be running around with every Tom, John, Sue or Mary, when your spouse doesn't know where you are or what you are doing. You can't go outside your home to be kind and do kind things, then come back home and all you do is raise hell, and promote discord.

Charity begins at home.

AVOID NEGATIVE CHARACTER TRAITS

Stubbornness-

This is the being rebellious, being bent toward doing things the wrong way, and not listening to the right way.

1 Samuel 15:23 KJV
For rebellion is as the sin of witchcraft, and stubbornness is as iniquity and idolatry. Because thou hast rejected the word of the Lord, he hath also rejected thee from being king.

Controlling Spirit-

This is ordering someone to do something, instead of getting up and doing it yourself. It is manipulating people to get what you want. Being bossy, pushy, and dictatorial.

Critical Spirit-

Putting other people first has become a problem, an extreme problem, even among the Body of Christ. The Bible says to take the log out of your own eye, before you try to take the particle out of someone else's eye. Matthew 7:3-5

Busybody-

Going from place to place, to get into someone else's business, or to tell your own business.

1 Thesaalonians 3:11 KJV
Now God Himself and our Father, and our Lord Jesus Christ, direct our way unto you.

1 Timothy 5:13 KJV
And withal they learn to be idle, wandering about from house to house; and not only idle, but tattlers also and busybodies, speaking things which they ought not

1 Peter 4:15 KJV

But let none of you suffer as a murderer, or as a thief, or as a evil doer, or as a busybody on other men's matters.

Gossiping-

Talking about other people's business, after they have trusted you to keep it to yourself. Or, trying to see the reaction from someone after you have told them someone else's business

1 Timothy 5:13 KJV

And withal they learn to be idle, wandering about from house to house; and not only idle, but tattlers also and busybodies, speaking things which they ought not

Nagging-

Someone tries to tell someone else what to do, over and over and over again. Just like a leaky faucet, no matter how much you try to keep turning it off, it just keeps leaking, more and more.

WHAT TYPE OF EFFORT
ARE YOU PUTTING FORTH?

A lackadaisical effort to put forth in a marriage, will end up as just another divorce statistic. Harsh words send a critical spirit, is just another step toward divorce. Pride, selfishness, arrogance, there are all the killers of a relationship.

The real question is, are you going to do it your way or God's way? If you take God's word lightly, the effects may devastate your mind and your life. The consequences are catastrophic for disobedience. God is not playing game with people, His rules are very clear and set for eternity. If you think you can sin and get away with it. Think again!!

Working together is never working apart from each other. If you can't pray together, or open the Bible to study together, there is a problem. If you are not on one accord, you are separated. You have to draw closer to God, so that you will be able to draw closer to one another. There has to be some discipline in your life to become a loyal partner in marriage. You have to go to work, clean up and pick up after yourself, because no one likes a slob. You have to take the initiative to get things done. Being obedient to God's Word brings blessings. Doing your own thing brings curses to you.

THINGS THAT WILL HINDER A GREAT MARRIAGE - SECTION 2

1. How Important is Sex in a Marriage
2. Satan's Warfare Against Marital Sex
3. Insecurities
4. When a Person Has Been Violated
5. Resolving Conflict
6. Marriage Stumbling Blocks

HOW IMPORTANT IS SEX IN THE MARRIAGE?

Anyone that says that sex is not important in marriage, is either being naïve, ignorant, stupid or just lying to themselves. Sex is presenting yourself to your mate, as a living sacrifice to them, laying aside all insecurities on the alter, to join as of for God's glory. It's not an unholy act, but an act of giving one's whole self to another individual for a lifetime. It's a consummation for your marriage to live for each other with God first in your lives. So even sex has a spiritual aspect, and that's why the scripture says certain things about our personal actions. This is a joining of two people, a spiritual partaking, into one, and as we read in:

1 Corinthians 7:2-5 KJV

2 Nevertheless, to avoid fornication, let every man have his own wife, and let everywoman have her own husband.

3 let the husband render unto the wife due benevolence: and likewise also the husband hath not power of his own body, but the wife.

4 The wife hath not power of her own body, but the husband: and likewise also the husband hath power of his own body, but the wife.

5 Defraud ye not one the other except it be with consent for a time, that ye may give yourselves to fasting and prayer; and come together again, that satan tempt you not for your inconstancy.

It's a sacrificial ministry of giving. That's why scripture says don't be joined with a harlot, its committing idolatry from the inside of your body.

1 Corinthians 6:16 KJV

What? Know ye not that he which is joined to a harlot is one body? For two, saith he, shall one flesh.

Many people are ashamed, for whatever reason, to give away (share) their bodies with their spouse. This prohibits any type of real intimacy within a marriage.

Giving yourself away, as to the Lord, cannot be taught by any human, only God through His Spirit can prepare you for service. This giving away is further emphasized when God says that each partner's body, belongs to the other person, we are stewards of each other's body. Sex is not to be withheld except for prayer and fasting, or by mutual agreement for a short period of time.

Marriage is all about giving honor, respect, submission, sex, love, compassion, and understanding, among other things. It's all about giving of yourself, for better or for worst. We are obligated to render certain things to our mates that are exclusively for them, just like we are obligated to God, because He has given us His mercy, love, and grace. We have gotten lazy about doing our duties toward one another, because we depend on other people to take up the slack for things we know we should be taking care of our own selves. For the family to survive, the husband and wife relationship has to survive. If you have not learned how to share yourself with your mate, your marriage is headed for a dead end. If we never look at serving one another, as also serving God we will never have the proper perspective.

One of the top allurements for men to sin, are women. Along with drugs, liquor, cigarettes and gambling are women. There is a constant assault on the minds of men, through TV, magazines, movies, newspapers, and even some churches, to commit fornication and lust after the opposite sex. Society is promoting that's ok, for women to step out into the world with little or nothing on. The programming of the mind can be so subtle, just like it was in the Garden of Eden. It's the easiest thing in the world to see a half-naked woman cross your path, but it's up to men that are committed to Christ to take a stand for the righteousness and holiness, to turn away to uplift Jesus Christ. Temptation doesn't mean anyone has to yield, even though there is a prepared deception to draw people toward the world. Society has purposefully set up hindrances to receive wisdom, knowledge, and understanding, by Christian rules.

Example 1:

Many people are pressed by their peers, toward partying and an active sex life, just look at your TV. Some are ridiculed if they are not familiar with every kind of sexual activity performed, from the days of Adam and Eve, until today. Many pride themselves for knowing how to do whatever sexual act that has ever been done by man or woman. This is why we have seen such things as homosexuality, lesbianism, wife swapping, orgies, etc., a no big deal. But the problem of sexually transmitted diseases and sin is being overlooked just to have a sex life. This is why unrestrained sexual activity outside of the marriage which is a big sin, and brings on judgment by God.

Example 2:

On the other hand, there are people who are uninformed, unfamiliar with and in many cases, unwilling to learn, about what they can do to maintain an energetic sexual relationship, by having an attitude of, "whatever happens, I must deserve it". You may also hear the "I'm a Christian woman, and I'm supposed to stay in my place and do whatever my husband tells me to do", I don't have a need to know any of that sex stuff because my husband does". Well, all that sex stuff is one of the spiritual bonds that helps hold marriages together.

But now we see, that is it just as tragic to know a little, and use it sinfully. One night stands are resulting in high rates of sexually transmitted diseases in the world. The ignorance of many things has not slowed down nor stopped the spread of these diseases and unfortunately all classes of society have very promiscuous activities outside of their marriages in today's self-gratifying world.

There are extremes that we can see between subcultures in our country about sex. Sex has been given a bad rap today. God gave sex to one husband and one wife to enjoy, but there are certain distinct mindsets from, social status to social status, to confuse the issue of sex.

Question? If wild sex is being promoted, why isn't it being promoted in the marriage, instead of everybody else in the world?

SATAN'S WAR AGAINST MARITAL SEX

This is the agenda that is being promoted by Satan:

1. Promiscuity

2. Sodomy and Lesbianism

3. Creating enmity between the husband and wife to pull the family apart.

4. Seduction of a generation by brainwashing (misdirection of minds toward lies)

5. Defamation of character being done by:

   a. Stereotypes

   b. The tearing down of morality integrity and values

   c. Fear (intimidation and control)

   d. Keeping people ignorant

   e. Distorting the thinking process to build up wrong conclusions (deception)

INSECURITIES

Quirks, bad habits, obsessions, negative attitudes, uncontrollable fears and emotions, lack of confidence (self-esteem), and all other negative characteristics that people have, comes from some type of insecurity of something. These insecurities are deep rooted and can become dangerous and possibly deadly.

In many people's lives, there have been voids left open somewhere along the way. Often, these openings are filled by satanic (demonic) influences. It could have been verbal abuse, abandonment, beatings, sexual abuse, emotional abuse etc., that has left that insecure feeling.

Memories of the past can be devastating if you let them. It can also lead to a state of taking your mate for granted. It is a great injustice to carry heavy baggage into your marriage, which has not been addressed. It's not OK by God's standards if your relationship is not lining up with His word. You are either in open rebellion or you need some help to get though these problems.

Some people have had wrong actions or reactions for so long, that now we think that it is alright to do them. It can be very easy to open up a gateway for satan to create wrong feelings and emotions. A few of the inappropriate activities people may have been involved in from the past or are currently involved in that could leave mental instabilities (insecurities) are:

Watching sexually explicit movies, with lots of profanity

Women or men who have been abused when they were very young

Following a wrong behavior that has been handed to you by your parents.

Unrestrained fussing and fighting with your spouse

Being involved in an adulterous relationship outside of your marriage

Today, our modern society is trying to make us believe that these type of things are okay, if the two people involved says it's okay. But the most important question is, what does the word of God say?

People are stressed out, confused and depressed. They turn to people who will give them a quick fix, or a quick answer and they usually contact a psychic, or go see a tarot card reader. They believe these people have all the right answers, and so they will spend tons of money just consulting them. They are looking to solve their problems the way the world does. This includes Christians that may have been hearing the word of God for years. We have to do things God's way, or we are just spinning our wheels and not going anywhere. We have to stand on the truth.

There are many people that have surmised that there is no other person in this world that could ever love them unless all the conditions that they have made up in their mind are perfect. How many perfect human beings or situations have you ever seen or know about today?

Lack of confidence (self-esteem) can be the result of many of society's pressures. If you don't look, act, talk, dress, or flaunt like the rest of the world, many times the people around you will put pressure on you to act like them, to conform to their ways.

We must acknowledge that we have a problem(s), and come to know we cannot solve them ourselves, but rather than trying to solve them ourselves to turn it over to Jesus. We have to learn to say, "I can't handle it Lord, but I know you can, so here it is." But you must leave the problems with Him to solve them, or work them out for you.

We have to give up on what the world says and hold on to what God say about you and who you really are.

Romans 12:2
1 Peter 1:15-16, 2:9
Colossians 2:6-10

We have to give all of our hang-ups, misconceptions, fears and wrong feeling over to Christ. He is the only one who can and will fix them. I know many people have bad memories of their past but Jesus is the way, the truth and the life. I know it hurts, but Jesus can take away the hurt, and lead you for the rest of your days on earth toward eternal life. Jesus is alive to make a difference in your life. Just like Jesus raised Lazarus from the dead, He can also raise you into a newness of life through the Holy Spirit. There is no quick fix to rid you of the pain you feel from your past, but if you want to have an intimate relationship with your spouse, you must place your trust in Jesus to reshape your life.

Bonding can't happen when there is a brick wall between the two of you, so therefore the brick wall must be torn down. Pray and fast like never before, for a breakthrough against the sources trying to rip your marriage apart. Be committed in your mind and heart and to your mate only.

Be aware that satan, the world system, and your flesh altogether will never make it easy on you to keep intimacy in your relationship with your spouse. These are forces that don't quit, and if they can capture your mind, the next step is to capture your heart. So what have you set up as a stumbling block to intimacy in your marriage?

So right now, hand all of your problems over to Jesus, confess your sins, and repent, to be set free.

WHEN A PERSON HAS BEEN VIOLATED THEY:

1. Live in fear and trust of no one.

2. Have feelings of:

   a. Insecurity

   b. Inadequacy

3. They can't relate:

   a. Emotionally

   b. Physically

4. They can't submit

5. They harbor feelings of

   a. Bitterness

   b. Un-forgiveness for past wrongs

6. This individual rejects openness:

   a. They are unresponsive toward any close relationship

   b. They can't express feelings (always holding back)

7. They talk a lot, but not about personal matters

8. They are unable to accept compliments

9. They can't grow in intimate:

   a. Friendship

   b. Relationship

   c. Communication

10. They have an un-surrendered heart:

    a. To God

    b. To any other person

RESOLVING CONFLICT

1. You will reap what you sow. Galatians 6:7
2. Your prayers will be hindered if you don't resolve conflict. 1 Peter 3:7
3. Never return evil for evil Romans 12:9,17
4. Edify one another. Romans 14:19, 15:2
5. Let love rule. John 13:34, 15:12
6. Don't let the sun go down on your anger 1 Peter 3:7
7. Watch your speech. James 3:12
8. Have mercy and compassion John 11:33-38, Luke 10:33-37, Matthew 9:36
9. Be able to hold your peace 2 Peter 1:2-10
10. Remember who you are in Christ 2 Corinthians 5:20, 1 Peter 2:5,9
11. Humble yourself before God. Matthew 20:27, 23:12, Luke 14:11, 18:14
12. Renew your mind daily (study the scriptures) Romans 12:2
13. Use the wisdom of God, and not of the world. James 4:14-17
14. Lift up a standard of Godliness and Holiness, keep your focus on Christ.
15. 1Corinthians 6:1-8
16. Stay in control(temperance) with a meek and humble spirit. Galatians 5:23
17. Take the time to negotiate and never intimidate.
18. Retaliation is never the answer.
19. Repent and restore your relationship, that means to rid yourself of selfishness.
20. Pray and fast for your marriage
21. Violence is never the answer, remember who you are in Christ.

MARRIAGE STUMBLING BLOCKS

In marriage, we have to try to avoid falling in a hole. We need to be informed about what is needed to continue a strong magnetism toward our mate. Developing a complacent attitude may also ruin our relationship. There are many things that may develop over the years, that could trip us up, and send us stumbling toward that ditch of despair.

Listed below are a few of these stumbling blocks:

1. Lack of discipline or self-control of:
    Anger, greed, rebellion, bitterness, lust, faultfinding, jealousy, ungratefulness, forgiveness, stubbornness, self-righteousness, impatience, revenge, retaliation, resentment, selfishness, stinginess, ungratefulness, sexual desire.

2. Lack of intimacy:
    We get into ruts of not being spontaneous in our relationship with our mate, not doing activities together as a couple, not having motivation to interact with each other. After a while, we tend to forget about romantic encounters and our dating life. Many start neglecting each other, taking the marriage for granted.

3. Fears of:
    Rejection, being hurt, criticism, failure, trust, intimacy, abuse.

4. Lack of commitment:
    No loyalty to your spouse, lustful, no foundation, unstable in your ways.

5. Lack of affection:
    Inability to cleave to your spouse, unresponsive or excessively restrained from intimate physical activity, not sexually responsive or motivated, taking sexual activity for granted.

6. Lack of self-esteem

    Not feeling attractive, not taking care of yourself, putting yourself down, depressive moods.

7. Lack of integrity:

    Unlearned about appropriate behavior, unable to make appropriate choices, irresponsible for your own actions, lack of knowledge of holiness or unwilling to practice it.

8. Accepting the world's point of view and morals (or lack of):

    Listening to the wrong sources, tolerating sin as a cover up for compassion, compromising the principles of God, for the world's principles (one foot in the world and the other trying to live for Christ).

9. Lack of communication skills and listening skills:

    No one pays attention to the other, and no one listens to the other, going on about their lives as if they are on their own.

10. Not encouraging your mate:

    Fault finding, constant complaining, lack of compassion, lack of caring, lack of patience.

11. Rebellious:

    Inconsiderate, negative attitude, not submissive, disobedient, stiff-necked, unthankful, hard-heartedness, stubbornness.

12. Lack of organizational skills:

    Men not taking responsibility as leaders in the home, women not being keepers of the home, poor stewards of finances.

13. Use of manipulation for self-gain:

    Trying to read people's actions, using your own interpretation of situations, using your mate in situations when you know it's wrong, misinterpreting Scripture (twisting it to fit your needs).

14. Not having quality time for each other:

    Using your spare time to do something for yourself instead of spending time with your mate, sacrificing something you need to do something you want to do alone.

15. Comparing your spouse to someone else:

Expecting too much from your partner, expecting the same personality as someone else, fantasizing about unrealistic expectations.

16. Letting your feelings always control your actions:

Whatever is done to you, you do in return, however you are made to feel, you give back the same feelings.

17. Wrong attitudes breed corruption

18. In the midst of a stronghold:

Not admitting to sin, not doing anything about sin, not being able to get over past wrongs, not submitting to God.

19. Your tongue can be a killer:

It tells who you really are, can and will create lies, it can lift up or tear down.

20. We can get wrapped up in vanity and world lust:

Pride, trying to be someone else.

21. Covetousness:

Must have what the neighbor, friend, or someone else has.

22. One or both partners causing divisions:

Out of ignorance or out of spite

23. Being a know it all/everything:

Not taking your partner's opinion under consideration, not even taking the Word of God as instruction or direction, not taking sources-other than your own handpicked ones as reliable messengers of God, no discernment, not Knowing the Word of God, well enough to apply it to your life, not meditating on God's Word.

24. Lack of submission:
    Humility not exercised

25. Lack of respect:
    No respect for the person, property, or words

26. Breaking of fellowship:
    Oneness, unity, feelings of rejection and separation, not being on one accord

27. Not being equally yoked:
    One is a believer, the other is not, not walking together as one.

28. Not letting your feelings be known:
    Fear of humiliation which bring on anger, tenseness

29. Misinterpretations of spouse's actions

30. Being laxed on rendering due benevolence to your spouse.

MORE HINDERING ACTIONS - SECTION 3

1. Selfishness

2. Rebellion

3. A Haughty Spirit

4. Stubbornness

5. Critical Spirit

6. Covetousness

7. Controlling Spirit

8. Unforgiveness

SELFISHNESS

Selfishness has no place in a marriage. If one person is focusing on himself or herself, they cannot focus on anyone else. This is the me, myself, and I generation. This is why we see so many divorces today, because one individual want everything centered around them. My way, my car, my house, my bank account, my, my, my.

The attitude of I am better at everything than anyone else, so I am going to take control of this relationship. This mindset is not going to work. If you are making God to be the center of your attention, this type of behavior will be eliminated. This is a killer of a marriage, when you are not working together. The whole relationship is separated.

Do not go into a marriage focusing on what I can get. Jesus said we must deny ourselves, and follow Him.

Selfishness is in opposition to the Christian life. Are you a person that is always thinking of himself/herself first and everyone else is just an afterthought? This is not the character of Jesus Christ.

Scripture References:

Romans 15:2
Matthew 16:24
James 2:15-16
1 Corinthians 12:25-26

REBELLION

This spirit is overtaking many of our families and our country. The Bibles says that rebellion is as the sin of witchcraft. Rebellion against people in authority placed over us, is an extreme problem in the world today. One probe is the figures of authority have a tendency to abuse the poser placed into their hands. A second problem is many people do not want anyone to be placed over them, to direct their way. So, we see families throughout the world, in turmoil because there is no leadership in the home. When Godly leadership is presented to individuals, many do not want to pay any attention. The rebellion continues in this generation without Godly principles. The leadership in high places do not want to hear anything about the Word of God. Most people want their own way instead of God's way, and never think about the consequences for their rebellion. God does not reward rebellious people, but its roots are growing deeper every day in our society. We can see the disassembling of the family and God pushed aside. We all need to come back to God, while we still have a chance. Men, are to be the directors toward God, because the family is your responsibility.

Scripture References:

1 Samuel 15:23
Proverbs 7:11
Jude 10-11

A HAUGHTY SPIRIT

This is what is referred to as high-minded, self-conceit, self-righteousness.

This spirit says, "I know that I am always right, and you can't tell me anything".

It builds me up, all the time.

Rudeness - Nothing is ever right what other people do in your eyesight. You tell everyone how stupid you think they are.

STUBBORNESS

Selfishness is not supposed to be a part of marriage, but two people are supposed to form one flesh and cleave to one another, which is a part of marriage.

When stubbornness inflates into total rebellion, it's like two magnets with the same polarities, not a chance of coming together because they are going their own way. You must humble yourself to be exalted. Stubbornness is refusal to hear God's voice. Acts of rebellion enslave people to sin.

Scripture References:

Proverbs 7:11

Judges 2:19

1 Samuel 15:23

CRITICAL SPIRIT

A critical spirit tears people down and degrades them. You tear something up on the inside of a person when you attack them verbally. You can never take back what has already come out of your mouth. It is abuse. Accusations and putdowns breeds' contempt, it sets up enmity, and breaks down any type of marriage bonds between couples. Demeaning or belittling your spouse is bad enough, but to do this in front of your kids or out in public, will tear your whole family apart. Remember, we will give an account of every idle word that we speak

Scripture Reference:

Matthew 12:36-37

There is nothing Godly at all, about putting people down. Attacks of negativity conveys dishonor, disloyalty, disunity, strife and contention. The conditions that result are stress, tension, conflict and rejection.

We have seen thousands upon thousands of cases of domestic violence, murdering of spouses, and murders of the whole family, because something snapped in a person's mind, when they were not able to take anymore abuse (mental, verbal, emotional). A critical spirit can destroy a marriage, and can open up the family to demonic activity. Satan may not be able to possess you, but he can bring havoc into your thought life. He can make you think that you are better than everyone is, and no one will measure up to your standards. That is the spirit of pride taking over and pride comes before the fall.

If you cannot build a person up (edify the), you should not knock them down. You are to focus on the positives about your mate, and give the rest over to God in prayer. It's our job to intercede, not to create a worst problem for our spouses.

Scripture References:

Matthew 7:3-5
Luke 6:41-42

COVETOUSNESS

Today in our modern society, many people use charge cards or credit to get everything their heart desires. Even to the point of bankruptcy, so they can start all over again. Some people may even use the lottery or the gambling casinos to try to make that big one hit in their life. Even to the point sometimes, of sacrificing their entire family to accumulate money for things, or maybe just for the thrill of pursuing the "big score". The world is telling you, "You deserve whatever you want in life", and they are going to help you to get it. God ahead, get that five hundred thousand dollar house, the boat, that corvette you always wanted. Go ahead leave your wife and get that twenty-year-old girl. Go ahead and live a little. These are some of life's biggest mistakes, which even church people are falling for. The overindulgence of appealing to the flesh is literally tearing families and this nation apart. We have made these things idols.

We see it on TV, we see it in magazines and we see it on billboards, get everything you want out of life. Who cares if God says it is wrong to accumulate things to keep up with the Jones's. Well, I care, and I hope there are other people who care also.

Scripture References:

Colossians 3:5
Luke 12:15

CONTROLLING SPIRIT

Many people get a thrill out of thinking they can control every situation, every conversation, the money, their spouse, everything. Isn't that the same way satan thought in Isaiah 14:12-15, when he thought he could actually be in charge of everything? Pride comes before a fall.

The world promotes people that they think can take control, but what does Jesus say?

Matthew 14:8-11, 18:4, 20:26-28

We must all come to a realization of who is really in charge of all things, because it is not any of us on this earth. If we all were in charge of everything in our lives, there would be no need for prayers, for church, or even any need to depend on anyone else for help.

Today in our society, we see a hardness, a harshness, in our women, that was not in God's plan. Many women fill as if they have been dumped on, so much by men that they are now going to be tough and be in charge of everything by force. That plan is out of order to God's plan, who has set the rules and is still in control. We have to decide if we are going to do the things God's way, or our own way, and pay the price.

Women, if you are not allowing your husband to be the head of the household, because you think you ought to be in control of everything, you are setting up problems in your home, with your husband, and your family. We cannot make people do right by taking over their lives or keeping them from what God has appointed them to do. Many times, we hold on too tight to our family members, to the point they become very rebellious. In order for God to take over, you must let go.

UN-FORGIVENESS

Holding onto un-forgiveness is like drinking a little bit of poison every day, until one day you just finally collapse and die. But every day you took the poison, you would tell yourself, this is only kool-aid, not poison like the label says, trying to deny that the poison is eating away at the insides of your body. This is what un-forgiveness does, it eats away at your body from the inside, and it will bring you down eventually. Denying that it is there will never solve the problem. Holding grudges and getting revenge is showing a lack of spiritual maturity. Jesus said we must forgive so that God may forgive us.

Scripture References:

Matthew 6:14-15
Mark 11:25-26
Luke 6:37, 17:3-4

THE CHARACTER
THAT BUILDS UP YOUR MARRIAGE - SECTION 4

1. Marriage Building Blocks
2. The Relationship that Women Attract Men Pursue
3. Men
4. Enthusiasm For Your Mate
5. Romance
6. Kindness
7. Affection
8. Sacrifice
9. Commitment
10. Compassion
11. Grace
12. Communication
13. Submission
14. Respect
15. Humility
16. Accountability
17. Contentment

MARRIAGE BUILDING BLOCKS

1. Exercise good manners

2. Exhibit grace and humility

3. Accept your mate as they are. Be satisfied with what you have.

4. Be spontaneous, enthusiastic, passionate, imaginative, creative, uninhibited, flirt with your spouse.

5. Be considerate, thoughtful and understanding. Be a positive influence.

6. Be a blessing and encourager. Complement each other.

7. Be affectionate, (if you don't know how, learn quickly)

8. Be consistent with aggressive closeness

9. Have fun building a bond

10. Cover for your mate. Do not let anyone belittle your mate, including yourself. Always edify each other.

11. Crucify the flesh. Self-denial is the only way to lift up Jesus Christ. You cannot always be doing your own thing and at the same time be doing the will of God. You cannot blab out whatever and whenever you feel like blabbing and expect God to bless it. Ask the Holy Spirit to help you to overcome an attitude of selfishness.

12. Men are to love their wives; women are to honor their husbands. These characteristics are learned by example that may be given to us by God. Men love your wives no matter what the situation may be. This is what brings about honor from the wife and God always honors obedience.

13. Never, never stir up any type of competition between anyone else and your spouse. Not even if it is only in their mind.

This includes your mother, father, siblings, friends, children, idols, and the list goes on.

14. Be open and honest with one another.

15. Be on one accord, remember you are one flesh. Start to be on one accord spiritually first.

16. Have mutual respect

17. Never lift up yourself, build up your spouse. Give up on self, to please your mate (within reason). Do not tear each other down; target the good qualities and not the bad ones.

18. Communicate your likes, desires, goals and what changes that would please you. We communicate through our attitudes, moods, body language, speech or lack of speech.

19. Find out each other's needs and try to meet them.

20. Assure your mate, you are always on their side, and trying to do what is best for them.

21. Be open to the truth always.

22. Learn what to say and how to say it. Learn when to talk and when to listen without interruptions. Put a watch on your mouth, you do not know everything all the time.

23. Focus on your mates strong points and pray about the weak ones.

24. Be a giver. Keep a sacrificial attitude of humility. Let love and peace rule. Self-sacrifice and humility can overcome pride.

25. Live as a forgiver. Live in grace and walk in love.

26. Have a firm grip on reality. Be accountable for your actions.

27. Remember that men and women are different and in most cases, will never think alike.

28. Learn to communicate effectively. It is critical that communication be consistent.

29. Keep yourself pure in all ways. The only one that is supposed to see your naked body is your spouse. Period!!!

30. Men make your wife feel safe and secure.

31. Women, be keepers of your homes. Honor your husband with submission, respect and sacrifice.

32. Keep God first, your spouse second, your children third, and other family and friends last.

33. Make quality time for your spouse. Make a date to get away from everything and everyone.

34. Stay in the scriptures. We are not governed by our own standard's but by God's

35. Pray with and for each other constantly

36. Seek the mind of Christ

37. Get a prayer partner of Godly council

38. Learn to know your mate

Remember what it took to get your mate, is what it is going to take to keep them.

THE RELATIONSHIP THAT WOMEN ATTRACT AND MEN PURSUE

A man needs to know if his wife is attracted to him, as much as he is to her. It is like some type of curse for a woman to tell her husband exactly what she likes sexually. The she will claim, "He is just not taking care of my sexual needs, so I will just walk away". Women don't have a problem conversing about anything else, so what is the problem with talking about their sexual needs to their husbands? The most famous quote from a woman to her man is, "you're a man you are supposed to know what I want". How really is a man to know when every woman is different? Men just cannot read the minds of a woman. If a husband does something his wife does not like then she is ready to cry rape. Therefore, if a husband feels like his wife is not interested, he then loses his interest.

Women, there is no big buildup for men to get ready for sex, but if you are in the mood and he does not know it, what do you think will happen?

Men all know women like to be touched in the right spot, in the right way, at the right time. But your husband must know where the right spot is and how to touch it in the right way, and the only way he will know, is when you the wife tells him. Going through the motions of getting ready to make love and there is no response builds up to a big letdown for both of you. Marital congeniality has never been an easy task to achieve, unless both parties are willing to complement each other.

Too many people are into self. What makes me feel good and if the other person does not know what I enjoy, I am not going to tell them. What type of relationship is this?

If the inner beauty is not acknowledged enough and if the inner self is not sanctified enough, and then neither will the outward character be satisfied. So being attractive on the outside is good, but being attractive on the inside by the Holy Spirit is best.

Remember the wife's body belongs to her husband, and her husband's body belongs to her.

Scripture Reference:

1 Corinthians 7:1-5

MEN

Men are logical, and nothing makes any sense to men unless it is logical. Where women use feelings and emotions, men use sight, smell, and stimulation out of the body to a greater degree. Many women have no clue on how to build up a man's ego, but they know how to tear it down. The main culprit of insulting and demeaning men is women's tongues. It is beginning to be very rare, for a woman to have any knowledge as of how to build up her man. Men do not want to approach a wife, which already has an attitude of being turned off. It is like women think more highly about attracting a boyfriend, than they do about attracting their own husbands.

In the bible, it says that the older women are supposed to teach the younger women how to manage their home and love their husbands. Well, for the most part, it is not happening in these days.

Scripture Reference:

Titus 2:6-7

ENTHUSIASM FOR YOUR MATE

Enthusiasm must be generated for your spouse. Whether it is in the bedroom, or just doing something your spouse likes to do. This works for husband and wife. If you seem to be not interested, your spouse will not be interested either. Sensitivity to your spouse's interest is critical. Learn how to excite your mate, let each other know what you like and what you do not like. Love is an action.

Your spouse wants you to be active in their life, without excuses. This is why many couples separate and go to another person for fulfillment and excitement, even though it is wrong. There may be another person who is energized, enthusiastic, and not hesitant to let you know what they like. If we would get this point across to the married couples, many problems would be solved before they could get started. Holding back from your spouse, for whatever excuse you may have, except for prayer is unbiblical.

Scripture Reference:

1 Corinthians 7:5

ROMANCE

Keep the flames burning hot? Do not take your mate for granted.

Be a blessing to them, have a special time set apart for just them.

Go on dates; buy nice gifts you know your spouse will enjoy. Teach each other what you like and do not like.

Women, wear your sexy clothes at home for your husband.

Men, find out what turns your wife on! (Good luck)

KINDNESS

Kindness comes from the heart, and if your heart is not right with God, there won't be any kindness towards others.

Only God can give you the capability to be kind, even to people you don't feel like being kind towards. Today is a day where kind words and actions toward others, is looked upon as being someone else's responsibility. The attitudes, the word, the actions, of an uncaring world, are overtaking even the church.

No-one hardly wants to go out of their way to show any kindness to others. It is really sad to see. Many people today want you to feel obligated if they do something for you, so at a later time they can come back to you and say, "You owe me because of the time I helped you." This is not God's Spirit. Kindness cannot be bought.

Scripture Reference:

Ephesians 4:32

AFFECTION

There seems to be a lack of affection today, from all members of the family. Mother, Father, children all have waxed cold. No wonder members of the family turn to someone else for affection, because they do not get it at home. An insensitive, coldness, seems to be the phenomenon that is spreading across this nation at a rapid race.

Your mate needs to know you want them as much as they want you. Drawing together, closer to one another through common interests forms bonds. There has to be tender loving care between spouses. If you let the spark go out, there will never be a fire. Caring means actions, kisses, hugs, whatever it takes. Woman make your husband look forward to coming home to you. Men, you cannot give your wife too much attention, affection, or love. Do things for each other without having to ask.

Scripture References:

Ruth 1:8
Colossians 3:2
Romans 12:10

SACRIFICE

No one can sacrifice anything, if they are into themselves. There are far too many people into doing their own thing, and not caring about anyone else. They cannot five up on what they want, to do what someone else might like. If only one person is doing all the sacrificing in the relationship, and the other person is only taking advantage of the other person, there is going to be a major problem. An unwillingness to sacrifice for your own spouse is a really bad sign for your marriage. You reap what you sow. If you don't put anything into your marriage, you won't get anything out of it. You have to give something to get something. Blessings don't come from selfishness, if you are not a giving person, don't get married. To be a living sacrifice for God, we have to give to others.

Servanthood is what we are called to do. This is what Jesus was trying to teach us all. For any of us to be someone special in God's Kingdom, we have to serve people now. It's a pleasure to serve because that is what Jesus Christ did, and we are to be striving to be like Him. There should be no problem serving our mate.

Scripture References:

Philippians 2:4
Romans 12:1
Matthew 20:27, 23:11
Luke 6:38

COMPASSION

The Bibles states that Jesus had compassion on the people, by feeling the hardships they were going thru and helping. Caring about what others may be going thru means that you have to reach out sacrificially, to help someone else, out of the concern of your heart. It means feeling people's pain and heartache, just like they do. Then reaching out to help with their circumstance or situation. Being sensitive to the needs of others and that includes your spouse.

There are several things we can say to others: "How can I help you? Or What are your concerns, that I may try to assist you? How many people do you show who will show compassion for others? Coldhearted people are like a cancer in today's world, and Jesus is the only one who can penetrate cold hearts. When you hear someone say, "Let me do this to make you feel better", is very rare is this day.

Scripture References:

Matthew 9:36
Luke 10:33
1 John 3:17
1 Peter 3:8

GRACE

Jesus knew, no man can have favor with God, unless their heart was changed to accept Him as Lord and Savior of their life. As He gave us favor, we should also give favor to our mate. Not through works, but through the Grace of God.

Remember when Jesus offered grace to the woman that was about to be stoned for adultery? (John 8:3) Remember the Grace toward Peter, even after denying Jesus three times, before He was crucified on the cross, (Mark 14:30). Also, remember how Paul persecuted the Christians, time after time before his meeting with Jesus on a road on his way to Damascus? (Acts 9:3-11)

God's Grace is sufficient for both God and men to extend. No one is beyond God's Grace unless that is the choice he wants to make.

The same can be said for married couples. If you extend grace and forgiveness to each other, when one or the other does wrong, you can strengthen your marriage, because you want to remain in your marriage and give it every chance possible.

Scripture References:

Ephesians 4:29
1 Corinthians 15:10
Mark 14:30
Matthew 26:34
Acts 9:3-11

COMMUNICATION

Communication opens the doorway to understanding. But men and women, always remember, your way of thinking, is probably not your spouse's way of thinking. When you communicate, make what you are saying as clear and plain as possible. Never think your spouse understands, and then find out that they don't. Most people perceive a lack of communication as a cold shoulder or rejection. We should never set up situations that may be perceived as a barrier of separation or isolation by your spouse. Spending too much time with your friends, activities, children, TV, hobbies, and other things or even a lack of touching, talking can all be perceived as rejection. You must grow to a level of knowledge to know how much time to spend with your mate for their satisfaction. But it starts with verbal communication, that's the only way you will ever know what the other person is actually thinking. If you get too caught up in other things more than your spouse, there is definitely going to be a problem.

The message you may be sending to your spouse, may be a complete turnoff to them. What you think is alright, may not be alright with them. You need to talk about the things that you want to do, and just make sure it is alright with your spouse, and try not to spend too much time when you do your other activities. Body language is a message; lack of interaction or intimacy is a message. Many time what you have said, may be altogether different in meaning to the person who is listening to you, then the message you are trying to convey. Many times marriage partners think that you are automatically supposed to know what they are saying, thinking, or exactly what they want. Warning! Don't fall for that, you will be sorry.

Communicate with sensitivity, and try to draw the total message. Make everything as clear as possible to get a proper understanding. Talk straight, be specific, and listen attentively.

We must communicate with a tone and in a way that is acceptable and honoring to your mate. We tell our children not to do inappropriate communication, but we do it with our spouse. It's not alright to nag, disrespect, or talk down to your spouse. There is far too much of this type of communication going on in families today and they often wonder why they have so many problems and why blessings are not being bestowed upon them. If you cannot speak to your spouse with love, kind and respect, you will have problems and you will need to seek help. Your first step will be to speak to your Pastor or Christian counselor, and absolutely seek God.

Our conversations should be taken as an opportunity to be a positive influence on someone else's life. We should try to know why a person says what they do without an interrogation. Listening is required. I guess this is why conversation is referred to as an art. You have to know how to create dialogue to pinpoint communalities. If the communication always centers around yourself, your marriage will soon be in trouble. Negative or sarcastic communication will pull you apart, not push you together.

Talking to someone of the opposite sex in a sensual, erotic, manner, other than your spouse, is committing adultery. You have to watch the way you talk to all people. There is appropriate speech, at the appropriate time. Don't let modern technology take over the time of communication with your spouse. TV, iPod, kindles, telephone, computers just to name a few are here to stay, but your spouse may not.

Scripture References:

1 Peter 1:15
Philippians 1:27

SUBMISSION

Most women cringe when this subject comes up. What does submission really mean? It means to let one person's decision overrule someone else's, so they can be accountable to God for that decision. Have you ever thought submission was like this? This is a command from God, for the wife to be submissive to her husband as being her head, like Christ is the head of the church. This is not a controlling spirit for the husband, but it lifts up the love for his wife by the leading of the Holy Spirit. So by this the wife yields to her husband's loving leadership.

Now ladies, you need to know that if you don't want to honor your husband as being your head, don't get married. You have no covering if you don't honor your husband as being your head. Which means you curse yourself if you don't repent? You follow your head, as he follows Christ. Don't marry someone you can't follow.

Sometimes submission may mean that you must humble yourself, to find out what a great blessing God had waiting for you, just because of your obedience.

There has been a lot of questions about what submission really is, because most women feel like this means putting on the ball and chains for their husbands. When in all truthfulness, it should be the man complaining for the responsibility that has been place upon him by God, because he must give an account for his family. Submission means that the woman states her views on a matter, and the man states his views, and if there is a difference of opinion, the final decision is given to the man to make for his family. But he also must answer to God for that decision. So, it would be to his best interest to try to make the best decision because he is being held accountable. A quiet and humble spirit is a major asset for a wife, to change the heart of her husband when God has given them a definite answer to a question. Men, if you don't listen to what your wife has to say, you may find out plenty of times that you have missed out on a blessing, because you were to stubborn to admit that she may have had a better solution.

We have got to recognize roles to understand submission. God the Father is the head over Jesus, Jesus is the head over the church, the man is head of his house and the covering over his wife and family. This means a willing acceptance of the ranks of positions, by grace. Then this extends into the process of mutual submission.

Scripture References:

Ephesians 5:21-22
1 Peter 3:1
Colossians 3:18
Hebrews 13:17

RESPECT

Many couples forget or neglect, to respect their own spouse. How can people show more respect to people outside the home? (Pastors, friends, teachers, doctors, bosses, etc.). I don't know. For a married person to continue to do their own thing as if they are not married, and without caring about their spouse's views or feelings, is very disrespectful. Cursing, and calling your spouse name, demeaning your spouse to everyone who will listen is disrespectful. You cannot preach your spouse into doing what you want them to do. How you treat your spouse is a true measuring rod, showing if God has any influence in your life. What are your actions saying?

If you don't stand up for your mate, and you join in on attacks on them, you are disrespecting them. Publicly demeaning your mate, may kill your marriage. What you think, what you say and what you do, is all a part of respect.

Scripture Reference:

Philippians 2:4-5

HUMILITY

There is a lot of lifting of one's self nowadays. But there was only one person that ever walked this earth that was perfect, and that was Jesus Christ. He humbled himself to be like us, and to be an example for us. No one is any better than anyone else, and God says to humble yourself so that he can exalt you. Pride is a killer. The I's, me's. and my's, will come to an end unless God has given the increase. Pride brings down the best of men and women, that really think that they are doing everything on their own without God's help. Pride says that you don't need any help from anyone else, because I believe I can do it all, because I am better than everyone else. It builds up me, myself, and I. Humility bows to other people's needs so that god can work through us so His work can rule in your life. Self-centeredness is fatal.

God will get your attention to let you know that He is still in charge.

Scripture References:

Matthew 23:12
Proverbs 16:18
Proverbs 18:12
Romans 12:13
1 Peter 5:5, 4:11
Colossians 3:12
Philippians 2:7-8
Luke 14:11

ACCOUNTABILITY

We all should give an account for every action that we make towards others. All things that are hidden in the dark will come into the light. There are consequences for our actions. When we are to make a decision that may have an effect on the family, don't just up and do something without discussing it with your spouse. If you have to make a quick decision and your spouse cannot be contacted, leave a note, email, voice message or something, to show that care about their feelings, and that you respect them. You have to think about how you would feel if your spouse made the same decision that you are making right now without you? If you can't tell your spouse where you are going and who you are going to be with, you are going to have a problem.

Scripture References:

Luke 16:2
Matthew 12:36
Romans 14:12

CONTENTMENT

We truly ought to be thankful for what we have, and not focus on what everyone else has. Every day is a true blessing, because God always provides us with what we need. Paul says that we should be contented in whatever situation we may find ourselves in. Only God can provide you with the peace throughout any storm that may rise. But to have a spirit of contentment, you have to acknowledge God as your source for all things. And we will then know God always has our best interest at heart. So if you are not content with anything, you need to look to God for your direction to learn to be content. What you have, and what you can get only comes from God.

Scripture Reference:

Hebrew 13:5
Philippians 4:11

FORGIVENESS

Holding grudges is unacceptable to God. He says if you don't forgive others, He is not going to forgive you. Your heart has got to be prepared by God, for you to be able to forgive someone. Otherwise, bitterness, resentment, hatred, and all the other negative attitudes are going to linger in your heart when you believe that you have been wronged. When you hold on to unforgiveness, it effects your health, your thinking, and your actions, and not for the better. God says to forgive, and keep on forgiving. Give it to God, because He is the overcomer, and only He can change your heart. When you learn to forgive, and are able to let go, you may remember what was done to you, but you can also count it as a lesson learned. Remember when God forgives you, He remembers no more, unless you do it again.

Scripture Reference:

Matthew 6:14
Matthew 18:21-22
Mark 11:25-26

CONTROL YOU MIND

Your mind is the battlefield of what your walk for God will get accomplished. We cannot believe everything that we hear, read, or even see. Deception is growing strong every day. We must be rooted and ground in the Word of God, or we may be fooled. Whatever is in your mind, will control your actions.

There are people and spirits in this world, that are in the business of capturing minds, to accept ungodliness as a way of life. Your mind must be alert to what is happening right now. Truth has never changed since the beginning in the Garden of Eden. This is a day of false messages, to lead the masses to hell if possible, Seducing spirits are out to capture minds if given a chance. There is no way that you can think like the world, and live for Christ. When there is no conscientiousness of what is right or wrong, the world is at a place for judgement. How close are we?

Scripture References:

1 Corinthians 23:16
Romans 12:2,8
Hebrews 8:10
Ephesians 4:23
1 Peter 1:13, 3:8
1 Timothy 1:17
Philippians 1:27, 2:2, 2:5, 3:16, 4:2

FEELINGS

Feelings can deceive you. One day you feel great about someone or some situation, the next day you are feeling indecisive. You may feel like this is the right person to trust about something, and find out that is really wasn't the right person after all. How can you overcome wrong feelings? By getting informed every day from the right source, God's Word, God's Spirit and God's wisdom, knowledge and understanding. Your emotions can overpower and sound thinking, and Godly behavior. Ladies, you know that your feelings are naturally enhanced by your hormones. Are your feelings controlling you, or is the Spirit of God? Feelings may change, but God's truth will never change. We are not to be tossed to and fro, but rooted in Christ. If your feelings are in opposition to the word of God, you are sinning. Feelings can be good unless they are out of control and out of fellowship with God. Seek God first, then He will give you the desires of your heart.

Scripture Reference:

Psalm 37:4

SELF CONTROL

In order for the people to be in control, they have to be under the influence of the Holy Spirit. It's not easy in today's world to keep your head together. Satan is planting thoughts to steal, kill, and destroy your life for God. We see the results every day, from people that are out of control. Brutal murders, robberies, kidnappings, mutilations, etc.., are a few results of people out of control. Most people that carry out these brutal crimes, don't even know why they did them. If you are out of control, you have no Godly power, and you are playing into the hands of the enemy. We have been targeted to be brainwashed by the world, to lift up the devil's agenda, and believe that is okay. An unstable mind is going to result in unstable conduct. The Word of God is the only way that you can maintain your self-control, in a world that has very little. The principals of God have got to be applied throughout your daily walk.

Scripture Reference:

Galatians 5:23
Proverbs 21:9, 21:19
2 Peter 1:6
1 Corinthians 14:40

HONESTY

Don't try to deceive your mate, or keep secrets. Lies will come out, and maybe sooner than you think. When you tell your mate, you are going to do something, make sure you do it, or let them know if something has happened so that you can't do it. You may create the effect of dis loyalty and/or a lack of sincerity if you don't follow thru with what you said. Being honest in everyway helps the relationship to grow closer to together and trust will begin to flow in your marriage. One lie will change everything. The first lie, depending on what was said, or covered up will make everything questionable in your relationship after that.

Scripture Reference:

Ephesians 4:15

Proverbs 21:6

TRUST

If you find that you can't trust your spouse, why did you get married? You must have confidence and assurance in your mate. If you have secrets to tell, get them out in the open with your spouse as soon as you can. There is no need to be embarrassed or ashamed because of something you have done. Remember the past always comes back to haunt you. Sharing is a part of marriage. If you can't share your heart with that other person, then just don't marry them.

Scripture Reference:

Hebrews 2:13
2 Corinthians 1:9, 3:4
Matthew 12:21

BEING GOOD STEWARTS

We have to use the provisions that God has provided for us, for His purposes. People tend to believe that the money we have made, is our money to spend any way that we want to. Clearly, we are in a day of self-indulgence, in which we tell ourselves that we deserve to have whatever we want. The real fact is, what we really deserve is hell, and I don't know anyone that wants to go there. God has blessed us to use what we have to build up His kingdom.

Covetousness is endorsed even throughout the church nowadays. It's called, "Name it, Claim it", prosperity gospel. The will tell you, "If you want it, just claim it", and God is supposed to obligated to give it to you. What a joke? I like what Jesus told the rich rule in Luke 18:18, "Can you give up your riches and follow me?"

Scripture Reference:

Luke 16:1

BE CONSIDERATE

It is really disheartening when you hear a spouse say, "I know my husband/wife would really like for me to do or not to do this or that, but oh well, I'm NOT going to change, even if God is laying on my heart to do so". There are some people who don't have to say anything, because you can see in their actions they really don't care about pleasing their mate. These incidents of inconsideration are saying, "I'm married, but I still have my own agenda, as if I'm not married." There is a real problem, especially in this country, with putting other's people's needs ahead of their spouses. And when we do find someone who will try to meet his partner's needs first, often times, the other partner tends to take advantage of them, or really are not appreciative of what they are trying to do.

There are many marriage partners that are being wounded by their mates with their words and/or actions. There are reports about vicious attacks made by marriage partners, both verbal and physical. Some of the words and actions coming out of the "so called saints", is as about as close to holiness as the North Pole is from the Sahara Dessert. When your spouse can't say thank you, or show any type of gratitude when they are given a blessing, something is terribly wrong.

Many people have gotten caught up in worldly attractions, more than they are in the Lord Jesus Christ, and their spouse. The major controllers that may be taking over in a person's life could be, your children, the TV, the job, friends, sports or social activities, social media, and even hobbies. Some people get so caught up, they can't even see their marriage dying.

We must be sensitive to each other's feelings and points of view. We must be patient in trying to understand our spouse. Remember, we are all misfits and imperfect. But you should be thankful for whom you have been blessed with. It you can't uplift one another, if we can't compliment and edify each other, then why even marry? Don't compare your mate with someone else, no two people are the same.

There are plenty of hard working men who go to work every day to take care of their family, that just could not measure up to their wife's standards and expectations, and they have been destroyed because their wife was a discourager instead of an encourager. Hurt feelings may result in a crushed spirit. You must learn how to encourage your mate and not tear them down. You should live a life of honor, respect, understanding, gratefulness, and compassion. These characteristics teaches you how to complement each other.

But on the other hand, there are wives who do everything in their power to please their husband, but the husband is never satisfied or grateful. A stay at home wife may cook, clean, wash, take care of the children, doing all the errands only to be put down, criticized or compared to what his mother would do. So, even if the husband is angry about something or someone, he must learn to be considerate of his wife as she is handling all the affairs and problems in the house that he may have peace when he comes home from handling all the problems outside of the home.

Scripture References:

Mark 9:50

Romans 12:20, 14:19

Galatians 6:2

Ephesians 4:2

1 John 1:7, 3:11, 4:11

1 Peter 1:22, 3:8

1 Thessalonians 3:12, 4:9, 4:18, 5:11

ENCOURAGEMENT

You can never build up another person and tear them down at the same time. It is difficult, in today's world, for a married person to help lift their spouse, when they don't even feel good about themselves. The is conveying to people it is ok to tear another person down, if is to your advantage and it benefits you. This is not what the Bible teaches. If you can't place a positive word in someone's life, it is best not to say anything at all. Compliments without hidden agendas, are almost a lost gesture in today's world. It's like we are supposed to put people down for their faults. If this were the case, we are all heading to hell, and Jesus would never have had to come and die on the cross for our sins. We should study Jesus on how to build up others. Philippians 2:3-4 says that we are to humble ourselves to consider others better than ourselves and to consider their interest. Building up others does not go unnoticed by God. Do something nice without being asked. This will make your spouse feel special.

Scripture Reference:

1 Thessalonians 5:11

WATCH YOUR WORDS

The words that come out of some of the husband's and/or wives mouth can be so very bad toward each other and it really should land them in jail. It is difficult in so many cases, and impossible to take back the words once they have been said. But understand, God is listening, and He is not pleased with the out of control speech. It's very easy to have a tongue that is out of control, saying whatever pops up in your mind. The quickest way to destroy your relationship is with careless words. It's not easy to have a tongue controlled by the Holy Spirit, but it is possible if you have decided that you really want it.

The brutal violence that takes place between a husband and wife always starts with words they have spoken to each other. Words that cut to the core are just not going to disappear, or just go away. Consequences come with disobedience through careless speech. An out of control tongue is like a tornado, where ever the tornado lands it leaves great damage, so does the out of control tongue. There is too much stabbing in the heart with harsh words. So be careful what you should say and how you say it. There is a way to be angry and get things off your chest without cutting each other to shreds. It solves nothing when the harshness of the words is what you are speaking to each other.

Scripture References:

Matthew 12:36
James 3:1-10
Colossians 3:8, 3:17, 4:6
Proverbs 15:1, 17:27

THE SENSATION OF TOUCH

Men, there are many ways you can touch the heart of your wife and so is the same for the wife to touch her husband. But most women have a greater sensation of touch from her man, than he will have. Husbands, you can touch the heart of your wife in ways that you never thought would mean anything to her. You can touch her body in the most tender of ways, that as a man you may not feel. Men, love and know your wife, her likes and dislikes, her body and all of her sensitive and intimate spots. You can set her on fire from what and when you know to do for her.

Ladies, if you husband is touching you the way you like, give him a response. Also, men if your wife is touching you the way you like, give her a response. This ensures that you are being pleased.

Sometimes, just hugging and kissing will make your spouse feel good and appreciated and loved. But whatever you do, make your spouse feel great.

INTIMACY

Get to really know your spouse by investing the time. If one person in the relationship cannot give of themselves freely, there is a big problem. You have to be able to share your heart about anything for intimacy to develop. Never be afraid to tell your spouse what you like and how you like it. You must get on one accord for the marriage to be blessed. Always consider the other person's feelings about situations. You have to have the freedom to be yourself at home, to be spontaneous and uninhibited. If you want to entice someone, make sure it is only your spouse. Present your body to your spouse as you want them to present their body to you. You have to develop an instinct of what your spouse wants at that special time. God wants you to bind together. But remember that intimacy is severed by deception.

Scripture Reference:

Genesis 2:25
Proverbs 5:2
1 Corinthians 7:1-5

STANDING TOGETHER

Cooperation means that both spouses are working together to solve problems. One person who is trying to control everything will lead to disaster. To be on one accord, you have to seek common goals together. One person cannot be going to the left and the other person going to the right.

There are individuals who are obsessed with being right all of the time. Don't get married if you think you are beyond listening to anyone else. When you think you are beyond the reach of being informed about something, you have lifted yourself up to God's level, and you are in a state of delusion. No one is that perfect.

Marriage is two people coming together as one. The challenge is to make it work for a lifetime. Sharing your life with your mate is a stipulation of marriage. We must create an atmosphere of bonding with one another.

Scripture References:

Philippians 2:2
Romans 12:16
1 John 1:7

SPIRITUAL HINDERANCES - SECTION 5

1. A Culture at Risk

2. Lack of Appreciation, Gratitude, Thankfulness and Consideration

3. Women Being Lifted Up

4. Spiritual Warfare

5. Illustration of the Flesh and Satan

6. Some if the Ways People Open Themselves to the Demonic Realm

7. Sexual Sins

8. Moving Away From the World

9. Bad Company, Brings Bad Results

10. Temptation

11. Keep Yourself From Idolatry

12. Don't Get Caught Up In Idolatry

13. Stay Away From Traps

14. Divorce

15. Don't Let the Devil Fool You

16. Familiarize Yourself with the Devil and His Demons

A CULTURE AT RISK

The "do your own thing" craze has got to come to an end, to be stable to lift up Jesus Christ as Lord. If we don't learn how to sacrifice ourselves for Christ, selfishness will always take over. But the "me generation" will die, one way or the other. If we need to be humbled for God to be recognized, you can believe it's going to happen. We have to learn to be obedient to what God has told us to do, and then He blesses us with the promises He has laid in store.

A marriage bond is truly a mystery nowadays, because way too many people want to do what they want to do, instead of what God has told them to do. Cleave to one another in today's interpretation means, cleave until I want to leave. That's not what God had in mind at all. If spouses let anyone separate them or come between them, they are sinning against God, (Mark 10:9).

There has been a constant struggle between the husband and wife for headship. There are women that even have religions that reverse any type of references toward men. They worship mother god Sophia, but God has placed man as head of the woman and the family, and it's up to the woman to obey what God has told her to do and to submit to her husband. But in these days, rebellion is promoted as being ok.

The Bibles says that in the last days, people will wax cold, living for their own pleasure, having no natural affection for anyone. And one of the main reasons for this lack of compassion is that there are no examples showing any other behavior. So, if there is no natural affection between the husband and wife, what kind of relationship is there going to be between the parent and child?

There is very little tender loving care from many women due to a generation of women's lib(feminist) movement that has taken its toll on husbands and children that end up confused, and have suffered tremendously.

In this day and time, many women are hard, and many men are soft. This is why our nation is in a turmoil, the men in charge don't have a clue, and they are taking bad advice from other people (especially women), that have a different agenda in mind other than honoring the constitution of the United States, or the Word of God. The rolls have been reversed with men and women, which is very much out of order.

Homosexuality is being promoted as an alternative lifestyle, instead of the abomination that God says that it is. Sensuality is being advertised everywhere, even in the children's cartoon. The mindset of many, are being captured by an ungodly onslaught of very organized attacks. Confusion has been targeted on the United States households by the enemy, and the family is on the downslide. Divide and conquer is the way satan has and is still working today. Confusion causes division, division causes selfishness, selfishness causes breakups. It's time for the children of God, to let God take control of their lives and to learn to be obedient to His word.

Fortunately, or unfortunately, women look for an example of manhood from their fathers. What type of examples have we seen in today's society, if we look at the home situations over the last thirty to forty years. A few of the negative influences on young minds have been divorce, promiscuity, drug addiction, incest, alcoholism, rolling stone parent, jail birds, child abusers, child support dodgers, and the list goes on. Are these enough poor role models to mess up a whole generation of young people? Well, almost! But now the lawmakers are trying to legalize such nonsense as pedophilia, banning of the Bible in every public place, the legal age of consent for sex at the age of 12, X rated TV on most of the TV stations any time of the day. Our society is promoting these things as being normal, ok, legitimate. How much more disgusting can a society get? Free love, do your own thing, what kind of examples have people been setting? Is there any wonder as of why the minds of our young men and women are so messed up?

Relationships have been blemished and distorted by spiritual elements at work to destroy the family and many of the people today are just going along with the program.

You can't leave God's rules of life out of your home, and expect everything to come out ok. You can't afford to direct your children toward a path of destruction. A whole generation of non-Christian (secular) programing, has had a dramatic impact on our minds, with a consistent brainwashing, of walking away from God. A generation where Christ has been replaced by pro-athletes, movie stars, music personalities, and prosperity. A stingy has even fallen on many of the churches.

There is no way possible for you to ever feel good about yourself unless you are living a Godly, righteous, pure, yielded, disciplined life. The only way you can live this way is through the power of the Holy Spirit, after you have given your life over to Jesus Christ. God has never abandoned man, but man has always been man abandoning God, and paying the price afterward. Just remember, God's truth is the only truth that there is.

LACK OF APPRCIATION, GRATITUDE, THANKFULNESS AND CONSIDERATION

There are many people today, who are so quick to find some-thing or someone better than what they already have. They think the grass is greener on the other side. People are quick to find fault in their spouse, and never anything good, often until it is too late. Being ungrateful is like an epidemic in this country. All people are special, but many today think that they have to throw other people away, just get tired of them and cast them out like you do garbage. Is your spouse's life precious to you? Can you express to your spouse just how much he/she really mean to you?

Scripture Reference:

Ephesians 5:20

WOMEN BEING LIFTED UP

A lot of people never realize that there are distinct differences between men and women. Women depend on their feelings to make decisions, sometimes, whether their feelings are right or wrong. Their emotions often overwhelm them, but women will not admit that they are weak in any way. Women are supposed to be right and in control, even when they know that they really are not. Women trying to take control, have always lead to problems. Now we have women who are military commanders, priests, bishops, pastors, congress women, and possibly very soon a woman president. The roles that God placed, are being cancelled against His plan. Women are marrying women, and men are marrying men. So, do we think that God is just going to sit back and have a little chuckle about these things? We have no excuse and we are once again, doing what is right in our own eyes.

Judgement will come, sooner than you think

Scripture References:

Genesis 3:1-6
1 Kings 18:4, 13, 19:1-3

SPIRITUAL WARFARE

Let me be perfectly honest with you. Satan does not want your marriage to succeed. He is out to steal, kill, and destroy through his deception. The devil will do anything to cause confusion in your marriage. Believe it or not, we are in a spiritual warfare. If God's Word is not obeyed, disaster will result.

Satan is not going to leave you alone, just because you think everything is great right now. He preys on vulnerabilities and weaknesses. He can create a question of doubt about God and His truth and righteousness. He can try to create a wedge between you and your spouse. He can create situations that seem hopeless. It's his job to try to capture your mind and attack your emotions. The lust of the eyes, the lust of the flesh, and the pride of life are his targets. Temptation will come, but which road will you take, the one toward truth and righteousness, or the one toward lies and deception?

ILLUSTRATION OF THE FLESH AND SATAN

Too many couples let the flesh take over and refuse to be a living sacrifice for God. But there are many different opposing forces hovering over the family today (even strongholds) waiting for an opportunity to slip in:

Satan's Demonic Attacks

1. Occultism-overexposure of T.V., Movies, games (tarot cards, Palm reading, Ouija boards, Psychics, etc) music, etc
2. Witchcraft
3. Paganism
4. Idolatry
5. Feminism
6. New Age Beliefs
7. Demonic Activity

Individual Fleshly Desires

1. Impure thoughts   Galatians 5:19
2. Lust Galatians 5:19
3. Hatred Galatians 5:20
4. Fighting Galatians 5:20
5. Jealousy Galatians 5:20
6. Anger Galatians 5:20
7. Trying to be first Galatians 5:20
8. Complaining Galatians 5:20
9. Criticizing Galatians 5:20
10. Thinking you are always right Galatians 5:20
11. Envy Galatians 5:21
12. Lying Revelation 22:12-16
13. Cheating 1 Corinthians 6:8
14. Adultery 1 Corinthians 6:9-10
15. Insecurity
16. Unforgiveness (holding grudges)
17. Gossiping (busy bodies)
18. Self-exaltation (non-submissive)
19. Lack of self-worth - (life controlled By feelings)
20. Unthankfulness
21. Ungrateful (coldness)
22. Worry
23. Fear
24. Bitterness
25. Addictions (drugs, sex, gambling)
26. Stubbornness

SOME OF THE WAYS PEOPLE OPEN THEMSELVES UP TO THE DEMONIC REALM

ACTIONS

a. Drug addiction (or other type of addictions)

b. Sexual promiscuity and perversions.

c. Alcoholism

d. Ungodly lifestyle (pursuing evil)

e. Being prideful

f. Justifying sin

g. Idolizing someone other than God

h. Being a man/woman pleaser

i. Being rebellious (disobedient) not obeying the word of God

j. Covetousness (greed) as are the gamblers

k. Passions (emotions) out of control, such as: hatred, anger, resentment, vengeance, fear, unforgiveness, uncontrolled tongue, argumentative

LISTENING TO THE WRONG THINGS

a. Ungodly music

b. False teachers (ungodly counsel)

c. Hearing voices just out of the air

LOOKING AT THE WRONG THINGS

a. Watching violent, sexually explicit, or occulted TV programs or videos

b. Pornography

c. Lustful concentration (magazines, TV, the beach, stores, ...)

d. Child pornography

SAYING THE WRONG THINGS

    a. Cursing at other people

    b. Taking God's Name in vain

    c. Nagging

    d. Stirring up strife and contention with idle words

    f. Lying

    g. Slandering

PLAYING WITH DEMONIC GAMES

    a. Horoscopes

    b. Ouija board

    c. Psychic hotlines

    d. Tarot cards

    e. Dungeons and dragons

    f. Charlie (contacting evil spirits)

DABBLING IN THE OCCULT

    a. Satan worship

    b. Practicing witchcraft

    c. Reading the satanic bible or other literature

    d. Using satanic signs and wearing satanic jewelry

    e. Playing satanic games

    f. Contacting evil spirits, the dead, spirit guides

    g. Praying or chanting to spirits other than God

NOT BEING ROOTED AND GROUNDED IN THE WORD OF GOD

    a. Tossed here and there, with every wind of doctrine

    b. False interpretation of scripture

c. Picking and choosing which passages of scripture you are going to obey, and which passages you are not.

SEEKING THE WORLD'S POINT OF VIEW AND WAYS OF THINKING

a. New age philosophy

b. Satanic brainwashing, mind control, and deception (being blinded to God's truth)

c. Being caught up in something more than time with God. The world says that all the beautiful people of the world, do this or that, they look like such and such, they go to this place or that place.

SEXUAL SINS

1. Lust – Pondering thoughts of having sex with someone other than your marriage partner

2. Fornication – Anyone having sex with someone that they are not married to.

3. Adultery – A person that is married and is having sex with someone else other than their Marriage partner.

4. Premarital sex – Having sex before marriage

5. Incest – A parent having sex with their child. Incest can also come from other family Members on younger relatives, such as uncles, brothers, cousins, father, mother, any Relatives

6. Statutory Rape – An adult having sex with a child under the legal age of consent.

7. Homosexuality – Sexual relations between persons of the same sex.

8. Lesbianism – Homosexuality among women

9. Polygamy – The condition of having more than one wife or husband at the same time.

MOVING AWAY FROM THE WORLD

The world seems to be overpowering large numbers of the so call, saints of the church today. It seems like it is a very difficult task, to walk away from worldly lust, that is influencing our day to day lives. To be empowered by the Holy Spirit, we have to make up in our minds that we are going to live for God. Worldly ways are the spirit of the antichrist. It is what the Bible refers to as, "doing what is right in our own eyes". If we really want to draw closer to God, we must abide in His will and His ways. Just because something feels good, does not mean that it is God's way. Our minds should be transformed to be able to stay close to God and His principles. Our lifestyle must reflect Jesus Christ as Lord and Savior of our lives.

What need to do to have the mind of Christ is to look to God for a kingdom mindset. To keep your focus on the Kingdom of God and not the things of this world. You will always be aware of your surroundings, but you just will not focus on them any longer. Your mindset always keeps you looking to God for direction and instructions. Let's face it, it may be hard, and you just might think that it is impossible. You are not your own, you belong to God. So give yourself the time and spend it in God's presence to be all He has created you to be.

BAD COMPANY BRINGS BAD RESULTS

The fact is, if you hang around a drug addict, you will at some time try drugs. What if you hang out with alcoholics, do you think you will be able to resist for long? Watch opposite sex friendships, your spouse will not tolerate competition. Competition is not what marriage is about. If you can't give your all to that one person, don't get married. Calling up that person of the opposite sex, to chit chat about personal things, or flirting with people that are not your spouse, or even setting up dates with someone that is not your spouse, is setting yourself up for big problems. If you have any type of friendship that is going to conflict with your marriage or your spiritual walk, it is best to leave them alone and walk away. Kissing and hugging on people other than your spouse, or family, be very careful, because there are people out there who don't want your marriage to succeed.

Scripture References:

Judges 16:4-21
Act 9:1-2

TEMPTATION

Temptation will approach you in thousands of different ways. And you should know, that satan knows your weaknesses, and he will use them to his advantage. Women are no different than men, both can be tempted. Never be so sure of yourself that you forget to depend on God for the only strength you may have, or you will fall. There is so much sensuality on display that is trying to divert your attention away from God. You have a choice but to turn toward the firm foundation of Jesus Christ, and go back into the sinful life, or stay in your foundation. It's easy to commit adultery, it's smart and commanded to stay pure. Flee immorality, flee programs or illustrations of lasciviousness, trying to capture your mind. Stay away from carnal people or corrupt conversation. What you see can hurt you, so be alert of enticements to draw you into a snare. Because once you have given in to sin, you can't change that particular occurrence. There is no time machine to take you back to change anything. We do have forgiveness of sins through Jesus Christ, but it would be to your advantage, not to get into certain situations, that would negatively impact your whole family, because of the consequences that you would bring upon them from your sin. You must keep away from carnal urges, just to make yourself feel good, however you can do it. God has always provided a way of escape from temptation. It's up to you to take it.

Scripture Reference:

1 Corinthians 10:13

KEEP YOURSELF AWAY FROM IDOLATRY

Keep in mind, that anything that you continue to keep your mind set upon, more than God and His word, is an idol. There are many things that we fail to consider an idol, when in reality they really are. A man may have a car, a sport activity or personality, he may have friends that he spends more time with than he does with his own family. People may tend to concentrate their minds on past relationships, the way a person was, what they may have liked about a person. Many women may concentrate on how she may have looked twenty years ago or before she had her babies. Fixing your mind on things like these, brings separation between a man and his wife, and also diverts minds away from the Word of God. If you can't concentrate on pleasing your mate because you are making other things, people or memories a priority, you have an idol in your life.

The relationship that a man and his wife is supposed to have, is like the relationship that Christ has to the Church. If a couple have any distraction in their lives, their relationship will not work and problems arise. The devil can use little distortions in your thinking to try to destroy your marriage. Don't deny your partner of their marriage rights because of selfish thinking controlled by the flesh, or because of hurt feelings someone else has placed upon you, or emotions out of control because of what someone told you twenty years ago. We can set up idols even in the ideas that we perceive to be right, according to your flesh. But what does the Word of God say?

If you have trouble concentrating on your marriage you have to remember who you are in Christ, and do what the Word of God says for you to do. It's not always easy, but we can do all things through Christ who strengthens us. Ask for help, and God will give it to you. If you set your affection on the things above, God can and will give you the desires of your hearts for one another. Submit yourself to God, then you will be able to submit yourselves to one another. Our focus has to become fixed on God's word and will for our lives. Satisfaction comes by overcoming lies and deception, and relying on the truth.

DON'T GET CAUGHT UP IN IDOLATRY

Who or what do you lift up more than God? Is your mind focused on godliness, or worldliness? Do you spend as much time thinking about how God has blessed you, as you about your favorite pastime? It doesn't take very much effort to capture your mind, heart and time. Lifting up a false god is not difficult at all. There are many distractions seeking your affection, to steer you away from God's plan for your life and your marriage. In today's materialistic world, you can easily get caught up in the glitz, and iconic worship of people. Many Americans have big cars, big houses, computers, cell phones, and more to redirect their focus from God. The false god you are worshipping could even be yourself!

Scripture Reference:

Exodus 20:4

STAY AWAY FROM THE TRAPS

Today, we are encouraged to do things that we know are wrong, because the appeal to the flesh is made to look like it is something that you just can't refuse. We even have churches today that say it's alright to have an abortion as birth control, it's ok to be a practicing homosexual or commit fornication or adultery, just as long as you have two consenting adults or you are practicing safe sex. WRONG! How about buying a lottery ticket, going to the casinos, or using the psychic hotline or Ouija board? How can Christians justify doing things like this? We have gone too far with being tolerant of sin by saying, "We are under Grace now, and it it's alright with me, it must be alright with God". WRONG again! It's not alright with God and it has never been, and everyone is not doing it.

It's not alright for men to go out with their friends for nights a week, and not expect your wife to be upset. It's not alright for women to go with their friends and get the charge cards maxed out to the limit, and not expect their husband to be upset. Couples, it's not ok for us to carry on conversation with the opposite sex, about what they are doing or what you are doing in your bedrooms, or what the spouse is or isn't doing for them. There are certain things about your spouse, that you don't need to be carrying on a conversation about with anyone else. If you do, you are setting yourself up for the adversary to come into your marriage.

Many marriages suffer from neglect: Sometimes people give more respect and honor to other people, than they do to their spouses. We say, "yes sir or ma'am", to the boss, the pastor, the neighbors, etc., and whatever they ask of you, you bend over backwards to try to do it. But your husband or wife can't even get a kiss, a good morning, or anything else. Partners have become too laxed toward the passion they should keep for one another. Couples just don't take the time out from the kids, TV, recreational activities, work, etc., to reserve some quality time for their mates. Many married folks are left to do the best they can by themselves. It's not good to do things for someone else, that you won't do for your spouse. It sets up bitterness and animosity. It is the trick of the devil, to try to break up families by getting them so busy that they won't spend time with one another to grow close in their personal relationships. It's not acceptable for the spouse to get into heavy emotional conversation, physical contact, or keeping their minds tied up with thinking towards other people besides their spouse. It's also not acceptable for a spouse at any time (except at the doctor's office), to overexpose parts of their body to other people.

When one parent makes a decision concerning one the children, it's up to the other parent to stand by them and the decision made, unless the decision is just totally ridiculous or unreasonable. Then, it's time to discuss that decision out of the child's ability to hear, to come to an understanding, Satan can work through your children also, as well as someone from the outside of your home, to break up the family. The favorite game children like to play is to play their parents against each other.

Fatigue is also a trap that hinders closeness to your mate. How can you have a relationship with someone if you can't even stay awake? Couples need to be involved in giving themselves to each other. Not just one, but both. We need to keep our health up, and make time for each other.

Being drawn into the trap of worldly lust, violates the marriage bond. The world's allurements can be so subtle and feel so good that your flesh and emotions can rule and captivate your mind and life, if you allow it. Sometimes, God will allow satan to slap you around, until you come to our senses, and be obedient to God's direction for your life. If you don't come to your sense, you may get slapped until the possibility of death may occur. But it's not God's fault when you are rebellious and disobedient, it's your own fault. You're never in a safe situation, when you create a lifestyle of sin.

Dishonoring each other in front of your children is one of the biggest mistakes you can make as a married couple. Why are your children like they are in this day and time? It's because they have seen mom and dad arguing, fighting, cussing and anything else they desire to do in front of their children. It is not a good environment to bring your children up in when you are supposed to be a Christian.

DIVORCE

God hates putting away, in other words, divorce. This is not man's loophole to get out of marriage the so called easy way out. Irreconcilable differences mean, "I want it my way or I'm walking out". When you break up a marriage, you are also breaking a vow to God. God will never tell you to get a divorce to make your life better. Breaking a covenant brings about unpleasant consequences. God allowed divorce because of the hardness of man's heart. It should break a man's heart to get a divorce, but it doesn't. No natural affection even for your wife or husband, what a day. There should be weeping for the whole family, for the so called, "easy way out of a marriage". It affects the children, the relatives, people's health and emotional stability, lifestyle, even their nutrition. There is no such thing as running away from your problems. Even in the church world, half the marriages think this is the easy way out.

Several things must you must remember about divorce:

1. It is not an option when you don't get your way.

2. It is not a way to get your feelings met.

3. There is no rosy outcome.

4. There are only three (3) legitimate reasons for divorce:

    a. One of the marriage partners commits fornication. Matthew 5:32

    b. The unbeliever wants to leave. 1 Corinthians 7:15

    c. The departing spouse want to remain unmarried or to be reconciled back with their mate. 1 Corinthians 7:11

Scripture Reference:

Malachi 2:16

1 Corinthians 7:10-14

DON'T LET THE DEVIL FOOL YOU

There are many people, who don't believe there is demonic activity in this day and time. They have seen so many special effects in movies, they can't tell the real thing, from what has been made up in someone's imagination. But believe it or not, satan and his followers (other fallen angels) are very real, and they are creating havoc and strongholds in lives today.

You can open yourself up to the demonic realm when you don't know the truth. Satan targets ignorance and overindulgences, to get your mind off of Jesus. Whatever works to turn your mind away from God, satan will try to use it. Satan comes to steal, kill and destroy, but only if you allow him to. He is a fallen angel, not God. The devil does have power, but it is only allowed by God to get your attention to focus back on Him, and it is very limited power that satan has. Satan attacks weaknesses not placed under the blood of Jesus. These are openings of vulnerability, which lead to captivity of the mind.

You say you don't believe that satan can capture minds? You could ask the people that followed Jim Jones to South Africa, if they were still alive. You could ask millions of Jews that were burned up in the furnaces, if they could have escaped Adolph Hitler. You could have asked Ted Bundy, if he wasn't executed for mass murder. You could ask some of the kids that were stoned out of their minds on drugs and listened to satanic music, that ended up killing their family, school mates, or committing suicide, because they heard voices that told them to do this. Satan has deceived couples into believing that if they don't get their own way, all they have to do is get a divorce to get out of the relationship. These are just a few examples of how satan can establish a stronghold on people's minds.

The devil is going all out to attack God ordained marriages and families. If he can disrupt families, he can create mass confusion in the world. So, as we can see, marital problems and family problems are spiritual in nature. Whatever way satan can help create a wedge within your family relationships, he is only too happy to do so. You say you don't believe in the devil or demons? Then you need to ask God to open up the truth to you about the principalities and powers, and also the battle satan has waged against God. Flagrant sinning is playing right into the hands of Satan's program. It gives him junk to work with to cause turmoil. Satan wants control of your life, through any means possible. He believes it is his job to break up unity and cause discord. Your weakness is his advantage.

But, what satan fails to recognize is that he has already been defeated when Jesus Christ died on the cross and was resurrected from the dead, and went to heaven to sit at the right hand of the Father. If you are saved by making Jesus Christ your Lord and Savior, and have confessed and repented from your sins by asking God for His forgiveness, and have also turned your life over to Him, satan has been defeated in your life also, but that doesn't stop him from trying to cause havoc in your life. Satan would rather for you to compromise instead of standing on the truth. Keep your focus on Christ, because He is in control of all things.

Being delivered is for believers who trust in God's Word, who may be tormented or possessed by satan and his demonic forces and also for believers who have left an opening for satanic forces to torment them. The blood of Jesus is the key to set God's people free. It is the cleansing power of Jesus Christ that will direct you toward repentance in your life. Then, it is up to you to line your will with God's will for your life. First and foremost, get saved, then be obedient to God's direction for your life. God is Holy, so we must be Holy and lift up righteousness in your life. God said in His Word that you were created in His image, so therefore you must want to live Holy unto the God. Sometimes, you will get off track, a doorway opens up for satan to walk through. The flesh is weak and you must learn how to control your weaknesses and desires.

But when you put your faith in Jesus, He is faithful to deliver you from all of satan's attacks. You can rid yourself of demonic torment, by being sold out to Jesus with fasting, prayer, and study of the Word of God, being filled with the Holy Spirit and above all, being totally obedient to the Word of God.

Satan knows the Word of God, after all before he was casted down from heaven he was there with the Father, so just know that he will take the Word of God and twist it, bend it distort it, or whatever he can to lead you away from God's truth. You have to seek the truth for yourself and stand on it.

My best advice to you, that is marriage partners and families, is to submit yourself completely unto God, because the devil is not your buddy. But he is playing for keep, he will kill, steal and destroy if you allow him to. Now is the time to run to Jesus, He is our refuge. Satan is going all out to drive you away from God, or from anything that has to do with God. It's amazing to see how a so called "saved people", let satan play with their minds and use them.

You cannot overcome, if you don't know how to defeat the enemy. Learn all you can about spiritual warfare, dig up information and learn all you can. You never know how the enemy will come at you so you must always be prepared. Come into the truth of the Word of God and stand on His promises to know that He is there for you always, and always have the open mind and willing heart to be obedient to God.

Which kingdom will you live for? God's or Satan's? There is only one person that can bring stability into your life and set you free from any and everything that is trying to take control of your life, and He is Jesus Christ, as your Lord and Savior.

FAMILIARIZE YOURSELF
WITH THE DEVIL AND HIS DEMONS

Isaiah 14:12-14

Matthew 4:24, 8:28-32, 9:32-33, 12:22-29, 12:43-45, 17:14-21, 25:41

Luke 22:31-32

John 8:44, 10:10, 13:2

Acts 19:13-16

1 Corinthians 5:5

2 Corinthians 11:3, 11:14-15

1 Peter 2:4, 5:8

Jude 6-7

Revelation 12:4-12

The Lord provides a way of escape:

1 Corinthians 10:12-14

2 Timothy 3:13-14, 4:18

THE LIFE WITH CHRIST - SECTION 6

1. Repentance of Sins

2. Being Obedient

3. Stay Focused

4. Follow the Word

5. You Really Do Reap What You Sow

6. Practice Growth in God's Spirituality

7. Personal Relationship with Jesus Christ

8. Exercise the Fruit of the Spirit

9. Jesus is the Answer

10. Walking in the Spirit

REPENTANCE OF SINS

What does repentance mean? It means to change your mind, and show a new direction in your life. To accept God's way and to give up your own way. But to really know God's way means you have to know His Word. Godly character cannot come from worldly sources. You need to make up in your mind that you are going to conduct your life in God's way. There has to be a brokenness to the way that you use to do things, and a new direction of truth and life everlasting.

So, the question is, are you going to line up with God's Word, or continue to do your own thing? Which direction are you moving? You cannot dismiss sin because worldly sources say it's okay. There are far too many people who are not making an attempt to live Holy. Not honoring the biblical statutes of the Bible for marriage is disobedience to God. Women are not submitting to their husbands, men are not loving their wives, are still violations of biblical standards for marriage. Don't just tend to overlook the sins of many may think are not really that bad. Those may be the sins that God may bring to your attention at the judgement. Your walk with Christ begins at home.

Scripture References:

Mark 1:15

Luke 13:3

Acts 3:19

BEING OBEDIENT

Right attitudes come from righteous thinking. Righteous thinking comes from knowing and applying the Word of God to your life, which results in right actions. Without know the Word of God, people tend to veer off onto their own humanistic way of thinking, which is where most of the world is today and sinking fast. God is the director toward goodness, not man. It's Satan's job to get you out of fellowship with God, so therefore, he needs to get you out of fellowship with your spouse. How can we say that we love God, and at the same time hate our mate? How can we be directed by the Spirit of God, when we are acting like the world? How can we love anyone outside of our home, when we can't love anyone inside of our home? There are ways that seem right in man's own eyes, that has meant the downfall of his own societies throughout history. God's Word must be obeyed, or judgement is always what results. Every word and every thought will be judged, and every action and the motive behind that action will be judged.

Rebellion is an act of witchcraft according to 1 Samuel 15:23. There is a lot of rebellion happening between marriage partners today. We tend to overlook the Word of God to get our own way. We listen to the wrong voices and they guide our marriages straight down the toilet.

If we would only do what God has directed us to do, we wouldn't have all the problems that seem to keep creeping up on us. We are supposed to submit to the truth. We are to honor God without speech, bodies, actions, marriages and everything else. But to do what God wants, we must place our faith in Him, in His Word, not in people. Men have nothing to do with making up the rules for us to live by. God has and will always be in control, and the rules will never change.

Satan is out to steal, kill and destroy, and many of us are just letting him have his way in our lives and in our marriages. A loving heart, a humble heart, a giving heart, is not what is being promoted in today's world. Tearing down and diving is what is promoted today. Addictions come about when our focus has been diverted away from God, and there is definitely a problem with addiction in America. Its's a spirit of gratification.

We have to got to be obedient to God's Word to be blessed, no straddling the fence or trying to justify sin by saying, "God understands that I'm not perfect", or "I'm under grace". Neither one gives anyone a license to sin, because God knows your heart and therefore know if you know better or not. There are still consequences for sinning.

We must make a choice to submit or not to submit to God's will. That's what is going to make or break our marriages. We have to keep striving to lift up Christ, by being an example and applying the Word of God to our lives. Feelings have nothing to do with having faith in God, or what He has given to us the truth in His Word. Repentance, consecration, meditation, and reaching out to others from the leading of the Holy Spirit, is what God intended for the Christian life. Holiness is a direction that saved people choose to guide their lives, it's a mindset, a decision as a way of life. It's not an option for us to live Holy or not, it's a command for the saints to live Holy because God is Holy. We have to stop being out of control, and become one under the control of the Holy Spirit. This takes brokenness by God to be shaped and molded into a person that can be used by God. God has to break us to make us. But if we are not obedient to God's direction for our lives, He can finally just leave us alone to do our own thing, and never use us for His service, ever again.

We have to stop setting our minds on earthly things, and start letting our minds be transformed by setting them on the things of God. This has to be done to prosper in Christ.

When you are withholding affection from your mate or not talking to them for long periods of time, to try to get back at them for not doing what you wanted or because they hurt your feelings, does not show any kind of maturity in Christ. In fact, this becomes a very serious problem in your marriage, that builds up into an unforgiving spirit and possible divorce. What if Jesus would have gotten back at the people that beat Him, or the Jews that brought up the charges against Him? He could have wiped out all of these people at any time, why didn't He? I'll tell you why, because He was an example for all of us, of the way we are to act with God's love. This is why we are called Christians, because we are to be followers of Christ, as part of His body, with Him being the Head.

We are to go from the old man to the new man, in order to know what to do and how

to do it. If we don't give our lives over to Christ, we won't be able to relate to our spouse adequately. We must renew our minds to be able to understand the ways of Christ, and to be able to put things in the proper perspective. After that, the Holy Spirit can mold and shape our lives into Christ likeness through brokenness. Peter had to be broken before he could be used, and so does everyone who follows after Christ.

We have to clean ourselves up and get on track with Jesus, or we will eventually see the discipline of God come upon your life. What are you holding on to that you have not given over to Jesus?

There is no slick way to get around or slide through the will of God. You either do what God says, and be blessed, or you can do it your own way and be cursed. It may even look like everything is going to be OK when you do it your way, but some day, some time, the consequences of being disobedient always catches up with you. There are no grey areas, in the Bible about any subject. Toleration or indulgence in sin will bring forth the chastisement of God into your life.

God is Holy and He wants us to follow His example. This is a wicked day where people are doing what they are treating as right in their own eyes. How much longer do you think that God is going to tolerate massive disobedience? God's instructions cannot be denied or rejected without consequences.

Scripture References:

1 Peter 1:14

Romans 15:18

Titus 2:5

2 Corinthians 2:9

STAY FOCUSED

There has to be order set by focusing in on the right perspectives. You can't do things exactly like your mother and father did things. They were human beings, too with flaws. I hear people say all the time, "That's the way my mother or father did it". But was it God's way? This spirit is overtaking massive numbers of people, even Christians, in today's world. Their minds are fixed on ideas that come from the past, whether they are Godly or not. What does the Word of God say, and if you find out that something you are doing is wrong, why keep doing it? If you are a believer, there is supposed to be only one way, and that is God's way. You can get off track if you have heard the wrong voices, and accepted the wrong messages. There is a spiritual warfare going on to capture your mind. The worldly mindset is becoming the norm for today, even in the church. This is a very dangerous state to be in.

The values of our thinking processes have shifted toward compromise of the truth. The breech of a Godly standard has been substantial. The truth is not setting people because they don't want it to. A true day of apostacy is right now. Can there be a change in the minds of behavior of the believers of today? We may have to give up some of old beliefs to be able to lift up the Spirit of God. We have to stay focused on who we are, and to what the Word of God is actually saying to us. There should be a difference within the thinking process of yourself, and an unbeliever. The Word of God should be taking root, and you should not be just putting on a front.

Scripture References:

Proverbs 14:12
Proverbs 16:25

FOLLOW THE WORD

You have to make up your own mind that you are going to do things in God's way, and not your own. The principles of God have to be followed daily to remain blessed. We have to study God's Word and take it seriously, for the Holy Spirit to be able to make an impact on your life.

We cannot afford to become stagnant in our walk for God. There should be no issues of compromise of the Word of God between spouses. Either you are going to follow the Word, or you are not. The Word of God is like a GPS unit for your life. Like the GPS, unless you turn it on and know exactly how to use it, the Word of God will be useless in your life. The Word of God will be a reliable source forever, to direct your life. If you are one of the people that are taking the Word of God lightly, there will be no excuse at the judgement seat of Christ for future plans.

Scripture References:

Acts 14:11
2 Timothy 2:15
James 1:22
Colossians 3:12

YOU REALLY DO REAP WHAT YOU SOW!

God's laws are going to stand, whether we believe them or not. The seeds that we plant toward people, will come back to us, sooner or later. I know that a lot of people will not believe it, just by the actions that they display. Most of the time, you can tell true believers from the world. If you treat someone like scum, that scum is going to come back to you. If you give a penny to someone in need, when you are able to give a lot more, you are only going to get a penny back. Sowing very little will not make you reap in abundance back to you. If you sow corruption, you will reap corruption. The world's standard is to make something seem acceptable, when it really is not. God sets the rules, not man.

Scriptures References:

2 Corinthians 9:6
Romans 2:6
Matthew 6:26
Galatians 6:7

PRACTICE GROWTH IN GOD'S SPIRITUALITY

Godliness isn't automatically injected in to us when we get saved. We have to ask God to give us His power to overcome those bad habits and behaviors, and to bring us under subjection to His Spirit and His Word. After this is done, we can continue to press on, under the power of the Holy Spirit, to be steadfast and unmovable.

This is the discipline required by god, to separated ourselves, to walk worthy of who we are in Christ, and to practice what we know is true. Every good characteristic you want to grow in yourself, and you want to come from your mate, all comes from the power of God.

Being Godly and pious at church, then acting like some type of demonic entity at home, will never fool anyone either. What is done in the dark, will always be brought in to the light. We have to be a living sacrifice for God, studying always to learn how to show ourselves approved. There is no stability in your life, without a proper respect for the Word of God and honoring it. After we do this, honor and respect will be developed for one another. Welcome Godly council and be willing to accept the truth.

Scripture References:

1 Thessalonians 5:15-23

PERSONAL RELATIONSHIP WITH JESUS CHRIST

You cannot help, or even relate to anyone else, without having a foundation of truth. There is no way you are going to be able to love your mate without God the Father, the Son and the Holy Spirit. There are too many nominal Christians, that do not have a real clue who Jesus Christ really is. Because of that fact alone, it should not be a shock to see the, "So called Christians", looking just like the world. There is an extreme urgency for Christians to know the real Jesus Christ. He is the King of kings, and the Lord of lords. He is the Savior of the world, whether you accept Him or not. The character of Jesus has been conveyed through His Word, and through the Holy Spirit. Therefore, there is no excuse for not know who Jesus is, and how He wants to direct your life. Jesus is the way, the truth and the life. John 14:6. Without Jesus, you are doomed to eternal damnation.

Scripture References:

Galatians 5:25
1 John 2:6
Romans 6:4-18
Colossians 2:6, 3:2
1 Peter 2:9, 2:21

EXERCISE THE FRUIT OF THE SPIRIT

Godliness does not come automatically when you are saved. You have to let the Holy Spirit work in your life. The Fruit of the Spirit, will only be manifested when you seek God daily. Christian conduct is character defined by an individual's acceptance of the truth of God. The fruit of the Spirit is the result of inner works of the Holy Spirit that dwells in you. And even then, that old human nature tries to take over by fighting God's Spirit. How many people are going to actually say, that it is easy to always display love, peace, joy, patience, kindness, goodness, faithfulness, gentleness, and self-control? I truly don't know of anyone who would say that it is easy. But the more we yield to God's Word, under the influence of the Holy Spirit, we will get built up to be able to live a Christian life. Not perfect, but drawing closer to God on a daily basis. Jesus said in John 15:4, to abide in Him, and then He will abide in you. Then verse 5 says that we will bear much fruit with Him and bear nothing without Him.

Scripture References:

Galatians 5:22-23

Romans 6:22, 8:1

John 17:16-19

1 Corinthians 6:9-11

Colossians 1:10

1 John 1:7

JESUS IS THE ANSWER

Jesus can change your life, and He can direct your path. His is the way of contentment in your marriage. So, trust and obey Him. There is a reason that god tell you the direction to go in every situation. There is no other truth other than the truth of Jesus Christ, the Son of God. Your role is "In Christ" for your marriage. Jesus said, "I am the Way, the Truth and the Life". John 14:6. So who are you following and making The Lord and Savior of your life? Will you stand on His Word and live for Him?

Scripture References:

John 14:6

Colossians 2:6-7

Romans 8:27

WALKING IN THE SPIRIT

Giving yourself away, a living sacrifice for God's service, is what the Spirit filled life is all about, dying to self. Study the life of Jesus Christ, what He did and the way He did it. The real question is, "how do I live a Holy disciplined life?" The key is, we must have examples, and Jesus is our number one example. Other Godly people inside and outside of our church are other examples. It's not easy for anyone to try to live a life anywhere close to Christ's life, but that is to be our lifetime quest. We must not only talk the talk, but we must walk the walk. The only way we can grow spiritually is to turn our life completely over to God (being sold out). Our mindset has got to reflect a lifestyle acceptable to God, not perfect, but striving to do God's will, and hating sin. That's the way we rid ourselves of the flaws and strongholds in our lives. We steadfastly become under the control of the Spirit of God, when we open ourselves up to be under the influence (yielded) of the Holy Spirit. But we must separate ourselves from worldly influences to be consumed by the Spirit of God. Self-control comes from daily discipline of being in God's word or in His presence. We have got to concentrate on how to be Holy and acceptable to God. Time with God, gives you the right perspective of everything in life when you are growing in the knowledge of God. If we don't study to have a discipline to have an affair, or to be a drug addict or an alcoholic. We have got to draw closer to God every day, or we will fall to worldly lust and pleasure as lifestyle. Also, the devil knows your weaknesses and where to attack your life, but if we stand on the truth of God, He will always bring us through and make us victorious.

Morality has already been defined by God, who has set all the standards, not man. Your performance of character begins at home with your family. But we have to stop setting our minds on earthly things, and start setting our minds on the things of God. Living in the Spirit brings us closer to Christ so that we can prosper in Him. But we have to take God and His Word seriously, or we will pay the price. If we abide in Christ, He will abide in us.

Scripture References:

James 3:15-18

Galatians 5:19-26, 6:7-10

Romans 6:4, 8:1

Colossians 1:10

Ephesians 4:1-3, 5:2, 15-26

1 Peter 4:1-3

1 Corinthians 1:10

Proverbs 16:32, 25:28

RESOURCES FOR FURTHER READING/ VIEWING

The Urban Alternative – Dr. Tony Evans
P.O. Box 4000
Dallas, Texas 75208-0560
1-800-800-3222

    Series: 1. The Christian Family
                    2. Divorce and Marriage
                    3. The Covenant of Marriage
                    4. Marriage God's Style
                    5. Roles in Marriage
                    6. Sex in Marriage
                    7. Sexual Purity
                    8. A Man and His Family

The Winning Walk – Dr. Ed Young
P.O. Box 3366
Houston, Texas 77253
1-800-350-9255

    Series: 1. The Ten Commandments of Marriage
                    2. God's Blueprint for Marriage
                    3. How to Understand Your Husband
                    4. How to Understand Your Wife
                    5. Sex in America

John Hagee Ministries
P.O. Box 1400
San Antonio, Texas 78295
1-800-854-9899

Series: 1. Sin, Sex and Self Control

Family Life Today – Dennis Rainey
P.O. Box 8220
Littlerock, Arkansas 72221
1-800-FLTODAY

Series: 1. Song of Solomon – Tommy Nelson
            2. Song of Solomon – Dennis Rainey

Grace to You – Dr. John MacArthur
P.O. Box 4000
Panorama City, CA 91412
1-800-55GRACE

Series: 1. Guidelines for Singleness and Marriage

Joyce Meyer Ministries – Joyce Meyer
P.O. Box 655
Fenton, Mo
1-800-727-9673

Series: 1. The Mouth
            2. Emotions Restored

BOOKS FOR FURTHER READING

<u>**BOOK**</u>   <u>**AUTHOR**</u>

1. Book of Romance   Tommy Nelson

2. Intimate Issues   Linda Dillow and Lorraine Pintus

3. Pillow Talk   Karen Liamen

4. Different by Design   Dr. John MacArthur

5. Two Becoming One   Don Meridith

6. Before A Bad Goodbye   Tim Clinton

7. The Black Family and Marriage   Melvin Hitchens Sr.

8. Sex Begins in the Kitchen   Dr. Kevin Leman

9. Do It Yourself Marriage Enrichment   Warren and Mary Ebinger

10. Marriage God's Way   Henry Brandt and Kerry L. Skinner

11. The Ultimate Marriage Builder   Dave and Claudia Arp

12. Daily Marriage Builders for Couples   Fred and Florence Littauer

13. The Five Love Languages   Gary Chapman

14. Secrets of a Fulfilled Woman   Dottie McDowell

15. Personal Holiness in Times of Temptation – Dave Wilkerson

16. Bring Home the Joy   Larry Crab, Dr. Kevin Leman,
                                                                 Les and Leslie Parrot

CPSIA information can be obtained
at www.ICGtesting.com
Printed in the USA
BVHW081513220719
554071BV00014B/434/P

9 781535 616997